THE
SEVEN
FAITH
TRIBES

THE
SEVEN
FAITH
TRIBES

Who They Are, What They Believe,
and Why They Matter

GEORGE
BARNA

BARNA

AN IMPRINT OF

Tyndale House Publishers, Inc.

Visit Tyndale's Web site at www.tyndale.com

TYNDALE is a registered trademark of Tyndale House Publishers, Inc.

Barna and the Barna logo are trademarks of George Barna.

BarnaBooks is an imprint of Tyndale House Publishers, Inc.

The Seven Faith Tribes: Who They Are, What They Believe, and Why They Matter

Copyright © 2009 by George Barna. All rights reserved.

Cover photo of fingerprint copyright © by iStockphoto. All rights reserved.

Designed by Stephen Vosloo and Timothy R. Botts

Published in association with the literary agency of Fedd and Company, Inc., 9759 Concord Pass, Brentwood, TN 37027.

Unless otherwise indicated, all Scripture quotations are taken from the *Holy Bible*, New Living Translation, copyright © 1996, 2004, 2007 by Tyndale House Foundation. Used by permission of Tyndale House Publishers, Inc., Carol Stream, Illinois 60188. All rights reserved.

Scripture quotations marked NIV are taken from the HOLY BIBLE, NEW INTERNATIONAL VERSION®. NIV®. Copyright © 1973, 1978, 1984 by International Bible Society. Used by permission of Zondervan. All rights reserved.

Library of Congress Cataloging-in-Publication

Barna, George.
   The seven faith tribes : who they are, what they believe, and why they matter / George Barna.
      p. cm.
   Includes bibliographical references (p.   ).
   ISBN 978-1-4143-2404-3 (hc)
   1. United States—Religion—1960- 2. Values—United States. I. Title.
   BL2525.B39 2009
   200.973'090511—dc22   2008050288

Printed in the United States of America

15   14   13   12   11   10   09
7   6   5   4   3   2   1

CONTENTS

ACKNOWLEDGMENTS

You'd think after writing more than forty books I'd have figured out the process and this one would have been a breeze.

Well, I haven't and it wasn't.

I'm not complaining, but this book was a bear to write. First, there was the massive amount of data to plow through and try to make sense of. Then there were the divergent tracks of thought regarding what to do about these seven tribes whose worldviews and behavior are so different. Add to that the sociopolitical realities of the United States—you know, the fact that the country is dying a painful death and nobody seems to have much of a solution. And, of course, concurrent to working on the book, the other dimensions of my life stubbornly marched on—our family (three teenage girls), my company (can you say "declining economy"?), the church I lead (pray, people, pray!), and other responsibilities.

So as you can imagine, being able to churn out two hundred–plus pages of text could not have been done in isolation. I am eager to thank those who encouraged me and made this book possible.

My team at The Barna Group, the research firm my wife and I started twenty-five years ago, has been stellar. David Kinnaman has run the company with skill and passion. He assumed extra duties, beyond his own insane inventory of obligations and opportunities, in order to relieve me a bit. Terry Gorka brought a laugh to my life each day while managing the details of our organization (and playing some great guitar licks). Pam Jacob crunched more data for me than you can imagine—and with a great attitude to boot! Celeste Rivera kept taking care of our customers without even complaining that I was sequestered elsewhere creating more resources for her to fulfill. Lisa Morter consistently did everything we asked and needed of her—and still had time to encourage me along the way. This is a great group of people with whom I am blessed to serve. I am grateful for their prayers and their partnership.

My church has been very supportive. Thank you to my good friends and fellow faith explorers: the Tice family (Tim, Tia, Josh,

Lindsey, and Whitney), the Woodruff family (Jack, Jana, Brenton, Parker, Nolan, and Carter), and the Schultz family (Bill, Amy, Ryan, Renae, and Janine). I am grateful for your prayers and encouragement.

My publishing partners have been terrific too. My literary agent, Esther Fedorkevich, has been a superb guiding light throughout the process. Esther's feedback and affirmation were crucial in the development of this project. (I do feel bad for her husband, Jimmy, who was made to suffer through various drafts of the manuscript. Thanks, Jimmy, I owe ya. . . .)

My friends at Tyndale have been wonderful as well. Those with whom I have worked most closely on the composition stages of this project have been patient, insightful, and supportive. This group includes Jan Long Harris, Doug Knox, Lisa Jackson, and Sharon Leavitt. It's gratifying to know that you are appreciated and prayed for by your publisher. It would be great if this book meets or exceeds their expectations: they deserve it.

Last, but never least, is my family. My wife, Nancy, has been through this drill many times, but she has remained married to me anyway. In this case, she juggled constant crises and challenges while I locked myself in the office to peck at the keyboard (yes, I type with two fingers). I don't know how she survived some of the ordeals that ravaged our family during this writing period, but she was a tower of strength and wisdom. In between handling family issues and ministry matters, she found time and energy to read (and sometimes reread) chapters or sections of the manuscript. Talk about enslavement! Must be love. . . . And my daughters, none of whom wants to follow in my footsteps (see: wisdom), were kind enough to regularly ask how it was going—and when I would finally be done. All of my girls gave up a lot of Dad time during the weeks when I was writing and rewriting this book—time with them that I will never get back. That is perhaps the greatest sadness to me about writing: the sacrifice of time and shared experiences with my children and wife. Lord, please vindicate their gift to me by using this book to transform lives and culture. Thank you, Nancy, Samantha, Corban, and Christine, for supporting and surrendering me for a while and then welcoming me back into the fold when it was all done. I love you all dearly.

PREFACE

I AM PROUD TO BE AN AMERICAN. This nation has an amazing profile of wonderful attributes and provides most of us with incredible experiences and opportunities. Having adopted three children from other less stable and fortunate nations, my wife and I are blessed to raise them here.

Like every nation in the world, the United States goes through cycles. During our up cycles, when things are going smoothly, we pay little attention to the long-term consequences of our choices and behaviors that could ultimately undermine the country's performance and potential. During the down cycles, we frantically rush to identify the problems that have brought about our decline and seek to repair the damage introduced by the careless or reckless choices of the recent past.

As we end the first decade of the third millennium, the United States is clearly immersed in a down cycle. The economy is unstable and in jeopardy. Our global relationships are strained. National security is compromised. Public education is ineffective. Marriage is on the rocks and on the precipice of being redefined, throwing families into turmoil. Natural disasters and an unpopular war are sucking vast amounts of money from our treasury. Old and new diseases are baffling our scientists and requiring record spending on health care. Traditional, Judeo-Christian morality is constantly challenged if not dismissed. Churches are struggling to remain relevant to people's lives. The political system is widely deemed to be broken.

But one of the greatest characteristics of America is its resilience. Consider all the challenges we have faced and overcome.

- There have been numerous wars in which Americans have sacrificed lives, money, and comfort, including the Civil War, territorial hostilities such as the Spanish-American War or the War of 1812, a pair of World Wars, a series of regional battles (Vietnam, Gulf War), and the ongoing battle against terrorism. We have come out stronger as a nation after each conflict was resolved.

- We have endured a wide range of criminal activities, ranging from the iron grip of the underworld on our economy during the first quarter of the twentieth century to the continual sale and distribution of illegal drugs.

- America has been beset by homeland unrest, such as the race riots of the sixties and the marches and demonstrations mounted by the civil rights movement.

- The nation has dealt with leadership crises, such as the assassination of presidents (Lincoln, Kennedy) and social leaders (King), the resignation of a disgraced president (Nixon), the indictment of various government officials, economic plundering by greedy corporate executives (think Enron and the 2008 financial bailout), and the passing of revered statesmen.

- Health epidemics have claimed many lives and dollars. Since the turn of the twentieth century, the nation has battled epidemics such as the Spanish flu (which about one out of every four Americans had in 1918, killing more than a half-million people, and dropping the average life span by more than fifteen years!), tuberculosis, polio, Ebola, and HIV/AIDS.

- Natural disasters have taken a huge toll on the nation. Floods, hurricanes, tornadoes, earthquakes, and fires have robbed America of tens of thousands of lives and billions of dollars that have been invested in attempting to rebuild that which was lost.

Incredibly, the United States has always fought its way back to health. We have remained a forward-thinking country brought together by shared values, goals, and hope. Our track record of bouncing back from hardships is a powerful rebuff to those who claim that the end of our stability and influence is at hand. In fact, research has consistently shown that nations, organizations, and even individuals can stay vibrant and powerful only by constantly renewing themselves. It's the basis of the popular leadership adage "What got you to the top will not keep you on top."

But America's history of rebounding from severe challenges does not insulate us from the need to address the realities that have dragged us into our current down cycle. Nations can only rebound when they intentionally seek renewal. And such comebacks, historically, have demanded that Americans either restore or redefine significant dimensions of the prevailing culture.

This book is about the renewal that the United States needs at this moment in history. The global nature of our world, along with the intricacies introduced by technological advances, makes such a retooling complex. Our need for restoration is multidimensional, requiring an economic component, a health component, a political component, and a communications component. The thrust of this book, however, is that at this juncture the most important component of all—the one on which all others hinge—is the moral and spiritual nature of American society.

Granted, as a Christian evangelical, I believe that obedience to Jesus Christ is the ultimate solution to all of humankind's problems. But I do not believe that the next step required to return America to greatness is the aggressive evangelization of the nation's majority. Should the masses embrace Jesus as their Savior, the nature of our culture could be radically transformed—but as our past experience has shown, having tens of millions simply accept Christ and then live in ways that do not reflect the values Jesus taught gains us little ground. In fact, a strong argument can be made that it loses ground for the cause of Christ as well as the good of humanity.

So this is not a book that will attempt to convert you and

other readers to my particular theological or spiritual understanding. The motivation for writing this book is concern over the inadvertent self-destruction of America. As you come to understand more about the seven dominant faith tribes of the United States, you will see that many of the answers to America's dilemma relate to rebuilding our sense of shared moral values and resultant community. The future of America depends more upon the compassionate engagement with society by devoted Christians than upon their persistent insistence of their moral supremacy.

I have spent the past quarter century analyzing the complex interplay between faith and culture, drawing insight from several hundred national research studies that have involved interviews with more than a half-million people. Based on that experience I am convinced that Jesus was right when He said that love is the key. Sadly, Christians in America are not seen as loving, but we currently have a window of opportunity to demonstrate our love in the midst of the hard times, confusion, and cultural chaos facing the nation.

Achieving positive outcomes, though, requires that Christians work in harmony with non-Christians—and do so without a covert evangelistic agenda. The best evangelism is that which emanates from people's respect for our character and lifestyle. Unfortunately, the public perception of our character and lifestyle is one of the major reasons why our evangelistic efforts in the United States have been so ineffective in the past quarter century. Those who do not follow Christ watch those who do and see little reason to follow suit. So rather than seek to honor God by doing more of the same, which has not produced much fruit, it is time for us to take stock of reality and reinvent ourselves—as disciples of Christ who love the world, rather than argue the world, into God's presence.

I believe that the most appropriate and effective means of doing so is by allowing people to make their own spiritual choices, with devout Christians simply peacefully coexisting with those who choose to believe differently. That can happen only if we mutually agree to focus on the things that we have in common rather than get ugly over the things that make us distinct.

In other words, we need to stop competing, comparing, complaining, and condemning, and we must start cooperating, communicating, collaborating, and contributing. It's time to stop fighting and start loving. It's time to stop taking and start giving.

This is a critical moment in American history. Everything is changing—and some of the most salient aspects of our existence are not changing for the better. At the risk of sounding alarmist—I despise manipulative marketing and hysterical rhetoric—I am convinced that our nation is in a major crisis moment, a genuine emergency that demands an extraordinary response. Even our leading politicians have sensed the challenge, with the recent presidential election emphasizing the need for change, rightly asserting that we cannot afford to continue business as usual. However, even the candidates missed the point: we do not need change as much as we need transformation, less in terms of programs and structures than in values and relationships.

And I hope this book will become more than a report of national ills. Ultimately, it is a call to action because you are a vital part of the solution.

If you love and appreciate America—it truly has been the land of people who are free and courageous, and has enjoyed a prolonged and unprecedented era of liberty and justice—then take notice. Please do your best to read this book with an open mind and a willing heart. Suppress your urge to deny that what is said in these pages is true and significant.

As I have so often implored the leaders I speak to, when you hear the analysis of our situation, your task is not to like what has been presented, but to demonstrate responsible citizenship by strategically dealing with it.

So join me on a journey into the heart and soul of America

as we plow through our nation's twenty-fourth decade. This is a tenuous time that demands your full attention, best thinking, and wholehearted commitment.

And I pray that in the end, you will join me and others as we struggle to help renew the heart and soul of this country—our country. Time is of the essence. We must respond quickly and strategically.

But only you can make that choice. Choose wisely.

Yours for America's return to greatness,
GEORGE BARNA
Ventura, California
January 2009

ONE

America Is on the Path to Self-Destruction

PERHAPS you have had the heart-wrenching experience of watching helplessly as a loved one—a parent, grandparent, sibling, or close friend—has wasted away due to a debilitating disease or accident. Maybe you have worked for a company that was once vibrant, profitable, and charging into the future—only to lose its way and go out of business.

The United States is in one of those moments. Unless we, the people, can rally to restore health to this once proud and mighty nation, we have a long and disturbing decline to look forward to.

Does it surprise you to hear that our greatest enemy is not al Qaeda or the oil cartel, but America itself? Such an audacious argument is possible, however, because we have steadily and incrementally abandoned what made us a great nation.

The elements that combined to establish the United States as perhaps the most unique and enviable nation in modern history can be restored—but only if we are wise enough, collectively, to focus on pursuing the good of society, not mere individual self-interest. It is this widespread drive to elevate self over community that has triggered our decline.

Some historians have examined the United States and concluded that it rose to prominence because of its world-class statesmen, foresighted Constitution, military might, abundant natural resources, and entrepreneurial spirit. Indisputably, such factors have significantly contributed to the establishment of a great nation. But such elements, alone, could never sustain it—especially for two-hundred-plus years!

A democracy, such as that in the United States, achieves greatness and retains its strength on the basis of the values and beliefs that fuel people's choices. Every society adopts a body of principles that defines the national ethos and fosters its ability to withstand various challenges. Only those nations that have moral and spiritual depth, clarity of purpose and process, and nobility of heart and mind are able to persevere and triumph.[1]

Achieving a state of internal equilibrium that generates forward movement is no small task. It has certainly eluded hundreds upon hundreds of nations and cultures over the course of time. A walk through world history underscores the difficulty of building and sustaining national greatness. Whether we examine the stories of ancient Rome and Greece, more modern examples such as the Soviet Union, Red China, the British Empire, and post-British India, or fascist experiments such as those in Germany and Italy, the outcomes are identical. After initial excitement and cooperation, each of these nations staggered into a dramatic decline, lacking the moral and spiritual fortitude to right themselves.

Among the lessons we learn from observing the demise of formidable countries and cultures are that a nation self-destructs when

- its people cannot hold a civil conversation over matters of disagreement because they are overly possessive of their values and beliefs and too unyielding of their preferences;
- public officials and cultural leaders insist upon positioning and posturing at the expense of their opponents after the exchange of competing ideas—even though those opponents are fellow citizens with an assumed similar interest in sustaining the health of the nation;

- the public cannot agree on what constitutes goodness, morality, generosity, kindness, ethics, or beauty;
- a significant share of the electorate refuses to support legally elected officials who are faithfully upholding the Constitution and diligently pursuing the best interests of the nation;
- people lose respect for others and refuse to grant them the measure of dignity that every human being innately deserves;
- the population embraces the notion that citizens are accountable solely to themselves for their moral and ethical choices because there are no universal standards and moral leaders.

Do these descriptions strike fear in your heart? They should. Increasingly, these are attributes of twenty-first-century America. Such qualities have pushed the world's greatest democracy to the precipice of self-annihilation. No amount of global trade or technological innovation will compensate for the loss of common vision and values that are required to bolster a mighty nation.

The dominant lifestyle patterns of Americans are a direct outgrowth of our beliefs. Operating within the boundaries of our self-determined cultural parameters, Americans live in ways that are the natural and tangible applications of what we believe to be true, appropriate, right, and valuable.

Therefore, we may not be pleased, but we ought not be surprised by the cultural chaos and moral disintegration we see and experience every day. Such conditions are the inevitable outcomes of the choices we have made that are designed to satisfy our self-interest instead of our shared interests. For instance, when we abandon sound financial principles and take on personal debt in order to satisfy our desires for more material goods, we undermine society's best interests. When we allow our children to absorb countless hours of morally promiscuous media content rather than limit their exposure and insist on better programming, we fail to protect our children and society's best interests. When we create a burgeoning industry of assisted living for our elderly relatives we don't have the time or inclination to care for, we redefine family and negate a fundamental strength of our society. When we donate less than 3 percent of our income to causes that enhance the quality and sustainability of life, our lack of generosity affects the future of our society. When we permit the blogosphere to become a rat hole of deceit, rudeness, and visual garbage, we forfeit part of the soul of our culture. When we allow "no fault" divorce to become the law of the land, as if nobody had any responsibilities in the demise of a marriage, we foster the demise of our society. When we choose to place our children in day care and prekindergarten programs for more hours than we share with them, we have made a definitive statement about what matters in our world.

Do we need to continue citing examples? Realize that all of those choices, and hundreds of others, reflect our true beliefs— not necessarily the beliefs to which we give lip service, but those to which we give behavioral support. And as we experience the hardships of a culture in transition from strength to weakness, we are merely reaping the harvest of our choices.

What has redirected us from what could be a pleasant and stable existence to one that produces widespread stress and flirts with the edge of disaster from day to day?

INSTITUTIONAL RECALIBRATION

A country as large and complex as the United States relies upon the development of various institutions to help make sense of reality and maintain a semblance of order and purpose. For many decades, our institutions served us well. They operated in synchronization, helping to keep balance in our society while advancing our common ends.

But during the past half century many of our pivotal institutions have reeled from the effects of dramatic change. Briefly, consider the following.

- The family unit has always been the fundamental building block of American society. But the family has been severely challenged by divorce (the United States has the highest divorce rate in the developed world); cohabitation (resulting in a decline in marriage, a rise in divorce, extramarital sexual episodes, extensive physical abuse, and heightened numbers of births outside of marriage); abortions; increasing numbers of unwed mothers; and challenges to the very definition of family and marriage brought about by the demands of the homosexual population and the involvement of activist judges.

- The Christian church has been a cornerstone of American society. But research shows that churches have very limited impact on people's lives these days.[2] The loss of influence can be attributed to the confluence of many factors. These include the erosion of public confidence due to moral crises (e.g., sex scandals among Catholic priests, financial failings among TV preachers); the paucity of vision-driven leadership; growing doubts about the veracity and reliability of the Bible; a nearly universal reliance upon vacuous indicators of ministry impact (i.e., attendance, fundraising, breadth of programs, number of employees, size of buildings and facilities); ministry methods and models that hinder effective learning and interpersonal connections; innocuous and irregular calls to action; and counterproductive competition among churches as well as parachurch ministries. Fewer and fewer Americans think of themselves as members of a church-based faith community, as followers of a specific deity or faith, or as fully committed to being models of the faith they embrace.

- Public schools have transitioned from training children to possess good character and strong academic skills to producing young people who score well on standardized achievement tests and thereby satisfy government funding criteria. In the process, we have been exposed to values-free education, values-clarification training, and other educational approaches that promote a group of divergent worldviews as if they all possessed equal merit. In the meantime, our students have lost out on learning how to communicate effectively, and they consistently trail students from other countries in academic fundamentals such as reading, writing, mathematics, and science.
- Government agencies have facilitated the acceleration of cultural dissonance. An example is the values-neutral admittance of millions of immigrants. Historically, immigration has been one of the greatest reflections of the openness of America to embrace and work alongside people who share the fundamental ideals of our democracy and are eager to assimilate into the dominant American culture. Over the past quarter century, however, a larger share of the immigrants seeking to make the United States their homeland has come ashore with a different agenda: living a more comfortable and secure life without having to surrender their native culture (e.g., language, values, beliefs, customs, relationships, or behaviors). Rather than adopting the fundamentals that made America strong as part of their assimilation and naturalization process, growing numbers of them expect America to accept their desire to retain that which they personally feel most comfortable with, even though it is at odds with the mainstream experience that produced the nation to which they were attracted.[3]

Our institutions have been further challenged by other cultural realities. For instance, digital technology—computers, mobile phones, the Internet, digital cameras, video recorders, and the like—has created an opinionated population that has become more narrow-minded and isolated even in the midst of an avalanche of information and relational connections.[4] That same technology has fostered an unprecedented degree of global awareness and interactivity within generations, while at the same time birthing new forms of discrimination and marginalization. Even the nation's economic transformation, moving from a world-class manufacturing nation to a country that consumes imported products and demands personal services, has altered our self-perceptions, national agenda, and global role.

ENTER THE NEW VALUES

The weakening of our institutions has freed the public to seize upon a revised assortment of values. An examination of the entire cluster gives a pretty sobering perspective on the new American mentality. As you will quickly realize, most of the elements in the emerging values set lead to the new focal point for America: self.

Consider the values transitions described below, along with the shifts in behavior that accompany the newly embraced perspectives, and ask yourself if any of them ring true.

From voluntary accountability to belligerent autonomy
Freedom traditionally implied that we were responsible to those whom we placed in authority—although we still had abundant opportunities to express our views and concerns, and to replace those whose leadership failed to live up to our expectations. In recent years, however, our perspectives on authority and accountability have changed to the point where many of us consider ourselves to be free agents, responsible only to ourselves. We resent others—individuals, family, public officials, organizations,

7

society—who place restrictions and limitations upon us, no matter how reasonable or necessary they may be. When people agree to be held accountable these days, such interaction is not so much about being held to predetermined standards as it is about providing explanations and justifications for the behavior in question, in order to produce absolution. Anyone who gets in the way of our autonomy runs the risk of being called out for such audacity and being cited for offenses such as censorship, fundamentalism, prudishness, narrow-mindedness, or intolerance.

From responsibilities to rights
From the earliest days of the republic, our nation's leaders accepted the notion that the freedom we fought for in the establishment of the nation could only be maintained if people were willing to accept the responsibilities and duties required to extend such freedom. Consequently, for many decades Americans have carried out the obligations of good citizens: obeying the law, supporting social institutions and leaders, mutually sacrificing, committing to the common good, exercising personal virtue and morality, and the like. To advance freedom, the health of the society must supersede the desires of the individual. But things have changed dramatically. People's concern these days is ensuring that they receive the benefits of the rights they perceive to be theirs. Standing in the way of such rights brings on threats of legal action; a lawsuit is now the default response to conditions that limit one's experiences. Ensuring the exercise of personal rights is the primary concern; exercising and protecting community rights are of secondary consideration.

From respect and dignity to incivility and arrogance
Historically, we have maintained that every person is worthy of respect and dignity. In contrast, increasing numbers of Americans these days are more likely to treat people with suspicion, indifference, or impatience. Americans have long had an international reputation for rudeness, but our levels of impolite behavior have escalated substantially in recent years. Beyond discourtesy, we

have become a society that is frequently and quickly critical of others. Rather than searching for the goodness in people, we are quick to point out their flaws and weaknesses. We have little patience with those who fail to live up to our expectations, and we have no hesitation in expressing our disapproval, regardless of the circumstances.

From discernment to tolerance

One of the most undesirable labels in our society is that of being judgmental. To avoid that critique, we have moved to the opposite extreme, allowing people to do whatever they please, as long as their choices do not put us directly in harm's way. In essence, we have abandoned discernment in favor of a self-protective permissiveness. This practice, of course, pushes us to the brink of anarchy, made all the more possible by our adoption of belligerent autonomy.

From pride in production to the joy of consumption

For decades, American citizens derived great satisfaction from the fruit of their labors and extolled the virtues of productivity. However, the source of pride now is in what we own or lease— the material goods that define our station in life and reflect our capacity to consume. In the past, a job was something that allowed us to add value to society and to participate in the work of a unified team. Now, growing numbers of people perceive their job to be a necessary evil, little more than a means to the end of acquiring the tangible items that may bring pleasure or prestige. As a result, the quality of our work efforts is seen as being less important than the rewards generated by those efforts. The hallowed concept of excellence has been left in the dust in our haste to embrace "adequacy" as the new standard for performance.

From contribution and sacrifice to comfort and fulfillment

Most Americans now perceive the ultimate purpose of life to be enjoying a comfortable lifestyle while possessing a positive self-image and a sense of fulfillment. The nature of one's contribution to society—i.e., what we do to advance the good of society—is thought of as a bonus, if any such contribution is made at all. People rarely consider it necessary—or even the mark of a good citizen—to sacrifice personal benefits or resources for the good of their community or nation, whether that is practiced through political involvement, environmentalism, financial responsibility, child-rearing practices, or other means. Unless such practices produce personal comfort and fulfillment, they are considered strictly optional behavior.

From trust to skepticism

Knowing that truth is not always considered a virtue and that truth is now widely assumed to be whatever the speaker defines it to be—regardless of the facts—Americans are more cautious and caustic these days. What used to be called healthy skepticism has now blossomed into full-blown doubt. Incapable of placing complete confidence in what we are told, we are reticent to trust others. Their motives (selfish) and words (misleading) must now be run through a filter that prevents us from taking things at face value, resulting in constant tension about who and what to believe. Rather than giving someone the benefit of the doubt, the default position is to reserve our right to remain skeptical. That same degree of mistrust has even diminished our willingness to believe religious teachings, whether from "reliable sources" such as the Bible or from other authorities.

From intellect and character to fame and image

Who were the heroes in years past? Often they were people whose intellect and commitment to improving the human condition produced value for our society: scientists, engineers, theorists, doctors, professors, and the like. Those people introduced life-changing innovations and solutions to our culture. They were joined in the winner's circle by parents, who were celebrated for their commitment to raising moral children and honorable citizens whose firm foundations of goodness would ensure the strength of the nation for years to come. Today these heroes have been unceremoniously replaced by a revolving door of simple-minded celebrities whose partying exploits, marital failures, materialistic excesses, relational squabbles, and fashion faux pas capture the attention of the tabloids and paparazzi.

We have traded substance for superficiality, intelligence for style, and hard work for merely showing up at hip locations. Celebrities hire image consultants to ensure that the appeal of their public personae extends their fifteen minutes of fame. They influence the gullible public to pursue unreasonable body shapes and expensive clothing, use incorrect or inappropriate language, and embrace dubious ideas about life. In the process, edginess, extravagance, and national recognition have trumped the values of character and intelligence.

From moral absolutes to moral relativism
Apparently, when Jesus Christ told people to "let your 'Yes' be 'Yes,' and your 'No,' 'No,' "[5] that was not what He really meant—at least, according to contemporary Americans. During the past quarter century there has been a massive shift away from the acceptance of moral absolutes (i.e., things are right or wrong, regardless of the situation) to acceptance of moral relativism (i.e., there are no absolute moral standards, so everything depends on what we each decide is right or wrong based on our own personal convictions and current situations). This has affected judicial decisions, government policies, business strategies, personal relationships, financial dealings—in short, everything imaginable. There are fewer and fewer situations in which conventional morality prevails. Life is now more anxiety ridden because there is no predictability or consistency regarding right and wrong.

Remember, we act out what we believe. Values form the core of our actionable perspectives. The evolution of American society is thus a reflection of this morphing of our values, changing everything about what we believe to be acceptable, valuable, desirable, and even holy.

THE NEW GOALS

This movement in our thinking and behavior has even affected our aspirations. As we dream of the future we will pursue, we've adopted a new set of life goals.

As recently as the 1970s, Americans were dedicated to becoming good citizens; raising children with proper character and morals; knowing and living according to accepted moral truths; experiencing and appreciating beauty in art and nature; living with integrity; supporting family members in all dimensions of life; and performing all tasks and responsibilities with excellence. The notion of living the good life centered on fitting into one's world as a productive, reliable member of a caring society.[6]

If that profile seems anachronistic to you, it's because our notion of the good life received a serious makeover. The dominant goals of Americans these days are achieving a comfortable lifestyle; having as many exciting or unique experiences as possible; feeling good about oneself; having ample options from which to choose in all dimensions of life; being able to participate in everything that is personally meaningful or appealing; developing and maintaining a positive public image; and avoiding pain or sacrifice.

You don't need an advanced degree to notice that the focus of our goals has taken a 180-degree turn. We are less interested in the good of society than in the promotion and protection of self. We are not as committed to making a societal contribution as we are to ensuring personal comfort and satisfaction. We would like to do well at our assigned or necessary tasks, but we are more committed to having great experiences and adventures than to fulfilling our responsibilities with certifiable excellence.

If you doubt the reality of this shift, talk to anyone who has owned a business for the past thirty years about the change in the dedication and quality standards of the workforce. Or you could speak to veteran teachers about the motivations of students. Try questioning marriage counselors about the nature of the conversations they have with adults whose marriages are on the rocks. Professionals whose work gives them insight into the nature of our culture will confirm the data that describe the reshaping of the mind and heart of America.

Another vantage point regarding who we have become—and are still becoming—is offered by people outside of the American experience. Sometimes we are too close to a situation to see it clearly; more objective perceptions are best provided by observers who are more physically removed from the situation. That's exactly what is provided by global surveys of attitudes. Several recent international research projects provided an outsider's view of American society. While the views of such people include various biases and assumptions—e.g., predispositions about Americans, our government, and our cultural preferences, all filtered through the survey respondent's own predispositions and preferences—the perceived decline in America's character comes through loud and clear. Europeans, South Americans, Asians, and Africans generally see us as insensitive, materialistic, self-absorbed, and superficially religious.[7]

THE WORLDVIEW REVOLUTION

Certainly, we have changed in meaningful ways. But no cultural transformation happens in a vacuum, and it is implausible that a national redefinition of this magnitude could have happened without some foundations being monumentally altered. In this case, the floodgates of our cultural transformation were pried open by our willingness to entertain—and eventually to adopt—alternative worldviews.

A worldview is simply the mental and emotional filter that each person embraces and uses to make sense of and respond to the world. Everyone has a worldview. Few have thought much about it or where it comes from, and even fewer can articulate the contents of their own worldview. But every person's life is a result of his or her worldview. And every nation's character is a product of the cumulative worldviews possessed and incarnated by its people.

In the 1950s and earlier, the dominant worldview in the United States might be characterized as Judeo-Christian. Most of the moral standards of the nation were based on Judeo-Christian principles regarding matters such as purpose, fairness, justice, value, goodness, beauty, relationships, family, generosity, evil, authority, compassion, and faith. While our nation has always had a multitude of faith groups and life philosophies resident within its shores, the past forty years in particular have seen the influx and acceptance of a variety of worldviews that are at odds with the historical foundations on which the country was built.

Because our worldviews direct our words and actions, this national transformation of our worldviews has changed life as we know it. Or, more correctly, knew it.

With the social upheaval that was ushered in during the sixties, everything was up for grabs—including the national sense of morality, spirituality, values, traditions, and lifestyle habits. To this day we are still experimenting and tinkering with our worldview: it remains a work in progress. But enough change has occurred that we can now see—and every day we encounter —the implications of this seismic shift in how we experience, interpret, and react to our world.

The bottom line is simply this: the substitution of alternative worldviews for the traditional Judeo-Christian version is responsible for America incrementally destroying itself. Gone are the days in which consensus was respected or personal views were maintained within the context of a different dominant worldview. Increasingly, we demand that the world embrace the worldview *we* possess or we respond in hostile ways: public criticism, nasty blogs and text messages, lawsuits, angry letters to public officials or professional associations, confrontational letters to the editor, damage to property, or other means of retaliation.

The element that facilitated a stable, consensual worldview in the past was the consistency of the religious beliefs of Americans. For more than two centuries, Americans generally held to some form of a Judeo-Christian perspective. Those who did not share such a perspective understood that while they could hold their divergent worldviews, theirs would remain a respected minority view. There was a recognized cultural accommodation in which the majority and minority allowed each other their space and respective social and political standing.

But even though four out of five Americans still consider themselves to be Christians, the prevailing accommodation has been scrapped as the proponents of each alternative worldview have battled for supremacy. Our long-held worldview moorings have been assaulted and have lost ground to alternative perspectives. The problem is not that a general lack of faith or absence of personal theology has undermined the Judeo-Christian worldview. The underlying issue is that those who normally would have defended and advanced the predominant worldview have succumbed to the lure of alternative perspectives that promise greater freedom and fewer restrictions.

This nation's spiritual beliefs are constantly evolving and morphing. At this moment in time, the fundamental beliefs on which the nation was founded are no longer the central tenets on which our country operates.[8] As we will see in subsequent chapters, basic ideals about God have been radically challenged, to the point where people no longer know what to believe and are warned not to speak in public about "Him/Her/Them/It." The idea of something being sacred—whether it be in reference to books (e.g., the Bible, Koran, Book of Mormon), beings (e.g., Jesus, Buddha), or places (e.g., Jerusalem, Mecca)—has been reduced from the extraordinary to the ordinary. The importance of following through on spiritual commitments, whether to God or to one's faith community, typically takes a backseat to other, more pressing commitments.

THE FAITH MIX: SEVEN TRIBES

To get a good understanding of the existing and evolving worldview mosaic, we must take a serious look at the dominant spiritual groups in America. I will refer to these as our faith tribes, based on the fact that the religious history of most Americans—Christians, Jews, Muslims, and even Mormons—describes the various segments of each faith as tribes. A tribe, after all, is a group of people who are united by common beliefs, customs, and traditions; who follow a common leader; and who consider themselves to be a community based on these shared realities.

Religious beliefs and convictions provide the central spectrum of ideas from which our worldview is developed. Getting inside the mind and heart of the major faith tribes will provide the necessary insight into how our existing worldviews came about, why we cling to them, and where they are headed.

Based on extensive segmentation analysis of the spiritual beliefs and practices of more than thirty thousand U.S. adults whom The Barna Group interviewed, we concluded that the United States is home to more than two hundred different religious faiths and denominations but is dominated by seven faith tribes. Naturally, each tribe has distinct segments within it that deviate from the dominant ways of thinking and acting, but these tribes, by and large, are cohesive masses. They range in size from several million to tens of millions of people.

A large majority of Americans are Casual Christians. These are people who profess to be Christian but are notably lax in their beliefs and practices. Casuals represent two-thirds of all American adults. There are variations within this sizable spiritual class, but overall the segment is surprisingly consistent in numerous dimensions of spirituality and in their attitudes and lifestyle choices.

Their counterpart are the Captive Christians—those whose consistently biblical beliefs and Christlike behavior validate their commitment to being followers of Christ. Captives constitute one-sixth of the adult population. They are characterized by a deeper, more intentional devotion to the principles and practices they embrace from the Bible. They are the segment within Christianity that is most likely to be caricatured by the media and by politicians, two groups that greatly misunderstand the motivations and objectives of Captives.

The rest of the nation is divided into five other faith tribes. Jewish people make up roughly 2 percent of the adult public. The percentage of Mormons is slightly smaller than that, though its adherents are strikingly unified in their ideology and practice. Pantheists—a combination of adherents to Eastern religions (Buddhism, Hinduism, Confucianism, Taoism, etc.), along with those who have adopted the American hybrid we think of as New Age beliefs—are also slightly less than 2 percent of the public. Muslims, while growing in number, make up considerably less than one percent of the American population, but they represent a significant, if controversial, point of view on the faith spectrum. That leaves the largest of the non-Christian tribes: the Skeptics. These folks, nearly 11 percent strong, are atheists or agnostics. They are, in essence, religiously irreligious.

We will explore each of these tribes in relation to key dimensions—demographics, religious beliefs and behaviors, self-image, attitudes and perceptions, lifestyle routines, morals, family realities, and political perspectives and patterns. These insights will enable us to delve into the various worldviews that Americans possess and then discuss how we can restore health to our republic. The required solutions are not political or economic. We need spiritual wisdom backed by a mutual commitment to live up to the chief aims of our respective faith perspectives.

BEYOND THE BEHEMOTH

You may be wondering what there is to talk about if one tribe alone—the Casual Christians—represents two out of every three Americans. By dwarfing all other tribes, isn't a book about the effect of faith in America really just a book about the Casuals?

Yes and no.

By sheer weight of numbers, the Casuals define the status quo. This group is, in a very real sense, the eight-hundred-pound gorilla that establishes the standards of the moral and spiritual life of the United States. In every respect, until something happens to intentionally alter matters, theirs is the default condition for the country.

To use a more familiar analogy, the Casuals are akin to the place of the Caucasian population in the United States. Each currently represents two-thirds of the population. Both groups are so numerous and familiar to everyone that they largely go unnoticed, but their significance is felt every moment of every day, whether we are conscious of it or not.

But in keeping with this analogy, recognize that they also represent a moving target for the smaller segments whose demographics, dreams, and desires are different from those of the behemoth. African Americans, Hispanics, Asians, Native Americans, and other ethnic and racial populations may be dwarfed by the Caucasian constituency, but they are never rendered irrelevant or powerless simply by being outnumbered. They simply have to try harder to get recognition, power, and favor in a country where they are minorities. And as our history shows, that is difficult but doable.

Is it truly possible for tribes that represent as little as one half of one percent of this massive country (i.e., Muslims) to overcome the standing of the group that encompasses 66 percent of the public? Absolutely! There are four significant reasons why small tribes have the potential to do so.

First, in a true democracy, everyone has a say. Sometimes even the tiniest voice speaks truths that others resonate with. With the prolific access to vehicles of communication in this country, and given the energetic defense of the freedom to express one's views, every tribe has the opportunity to make its case.

Second, influence is often magnified through dynamic partnerships in which multiple minor players coordinate their efforts to exert impact that transcends their numbers. The mosaic of our population is increasingly characterized by connections across lines—racial, political, economic, religious, and geographic. It is common these days to see coalitions of groups that have never before worked together to break through preexisting barriers to jointly pursue outcomes that are important to all of them.

Third, one of the most powerful ways of influencing today's population is through modeling. People learn by example. Habits and predispositions are challenged by example. Trends are ignited by a relative handful of people who do something that grabs attention and generates interest.

Fourth, and perhaps most important, never underestimate the power of passion. Groups pursuing outcomes that they are willing to fight for with every resource they can muster often generate results far beyond the expectations of those who observe their battle with indifference or amusement.

For example, if it were up to the white majority during the middle of the last century, the African American community would still be living in segregated neighborhoods and dealing with a network of isolated social institutions, working for substandard pay in untenable conditions. During the civil rights movement of the sixties and seventies, the African American population was a mere one out of every ten Americans. In terms of raw numbers, they had little hope of changing the mores of this nation.

But because the United States is a democracy whose Constitution promises all people specific rights that give them a place at the table and the right to pursue their dreams, African Americans had a chance to change the larger social context. Through the strategic deployment of various legal means—such as peaceful demonstrations, political lobbying, media influence, boycotts, and prayer—they were able to make their case to the public and to work through the political system. They created viable partnerships with a broad coalition of external groups—churches, other minority populations, various political groups, and associations—to advance their cause. And they were able to defeat overwhelming odds, and endure great injustices en route, to gain ground. African Americans stood firmly behind their leaders and refused to back down, even when it meant physical pain or other personal hardships. Their unflagging passion, directed by brilliant leaders and channeled through the sacrificial participation of a relative handful of African American people, enabled them to rewrite the well-established norms of a global superpower.

A current example of how a minuscule group can have a big voice in a cacophonous society is the experience of the gay community. Although gay people are no more than 3 percent to 5 percent of the adult population, the nation is in tumult over their demands for marriage rights and other changes in policies that affect their lives. Taking a page from the playbook of the civil rights movement, the gay population has used the freedoms and rights provided by the Constitution to its advantage, enabling its members to get the public's attention and persuade an increasingly sympathetic society to see things their way. Tens of millions of Americans who will never engage in or even consider embracing homosexual behaviors are nevertheless leaning toward or fully supportive of an array of new laws and policies that will satisfy the desires of the gay movement.

Sometimes the giant is vulnerable to the midget. The giant takes such great comfort in its size that it ignores or dismisses things that will eventually return to haunt it. And sometimes the same magnitude that has given the giant reason for comfort becomes the very attribute that disables the behemoth from responding in a timely, strategic, or otherwise effective manner.

THE ABSENCE OF RELIGIOUS FREEDOM

An inescapable fact of our society is that the vast majority of Americans are connected to Christianity to some degree. And yet, as further testimony to the fact that size is not everything, one of the disturbing conditions in present-day America is that no tribe—not even the Casual or Captive Christians—is allowed to freely pursue its faith without undue interference.

Like all faith tribes, Christian-based tribes must satisfy certain cultural requirements in order to live in a Christlike manner, which is their core spiritual mandate. Among those are to consistently worship their God, to obey His commands as outlined in the Bible, to serve God and people in meaningful ways, and to generously give and receive love. The nation's democracy was supposed to provide such opportunities to the Christians who sacrificed so much to establish the United States. The desire to experience such freedoms was one of the precipitating motivations for establishing independence from British rule.

Some readers will be surprised to hear that the Christian-based tribes in the United States do not currently have those freedoms and abilities. Similarly, in a country that is predicated upon delivering specified rights and their attendant freedoms to all of its citizens, other faith tribes suffer the indignity and injustice of being prevented from exercising those rights as their faith would lead them to.

If you doubt this, please read the biology textbooks used in many government-funded (i.e., public) schools, which make no bones about critiquing Christianity, eliminating faith-based views in favor of science-based explanations, or promoting "safe sex" rather than the biblical alternative of sexual abstinence. Consider the implications of laws that diminish the value of human life or redefine the biblical standard of marriage. Take note of government threats to, or restrictions on, families that homeschool their children for moral or religious reasons. Think about the implication of laws requiring Christian ministries to hire employees who reject their beliefs or who practice lifestyles that visibly and unapologetically conflict with the moral convictions of the ministry. Talk to Christian graduate students around the nation and discover how many of them jeopardize their advanced degrees or scholarly careers if they admit to believing in creationism. How many high school graduation speeches were altered this year by laws preventing students from incorporating their religious beliefs into their remarks? In certain states, Bibles are not allowed in the public school classroom.

These are but a handful of the incendiary examples of how the religious freedoms of just one of the tribes are trampled in the alleged interest of freedom. How we handle these issues has consistently divided the tribes within our country.

NOT SEEKING A THEOCRACY

Please do not miss where I'm headed with this argument. America was not meant to be a theocracy—that is, ruled by a given religious tribe. The dominant spiritual classes in our society should neither possess nor expect to have the final say on all legal and moral matters. In fact, our research consistently shows that Christians in America appreciate their neighbors who belong to other faith tribes; they simply do not want their own ability to serve their God limited by the discomfort or desires of those other tribes any more than the minority tribes want their freedoms to be limited or negated by the larger tribal groups.

In an odd way we have reached a stalemate. Significantly, our research indicates that the United States is presently a nation in which

- none of our faith tribes feel they are able to freely practice their faith without breaking laws or upsetting members of other tribes;
- each tribe feels that the other tribes do not understand what their faith is about and that they cannot get other tribes to give them a fair hearing;
- the freedoms of tribes to practice their faith and hold their particular beliefs are being eliminated by whichever tribe outmaneuvers the others within the political and legal arenas;
- tribal leadership has become more about political prowess exercised in the public domain than about the

provision of spiritual and moral guidance within the
confines of the tribe;

- people's inability to experience the religious freedom
guaranteed under the Constitution is causing them
to feel as if the nation is losing its heart and soul, and
along with that, its greatness.

The problem facing America is not the presence of divergent
faith tribes. For many years, the United States has had a diverse
spiritual palette—and has been one of the most revered and successful nations on earth because of it. The experience of other
nations further confirms that being home to multiple faith tribes
is not necessarily an issue. In fact, one could make a compelling
argument that it is healthy to have a variety of faith perspectives resident in the same marketplace of ideas and lifestyles.
Faith tribes need not be adversarial; religious conflict is not so
much an inevitable product of the differing principles of each
tribe as it is a reflection of other values and factors driving the
mother culture.

As we witness the deterioration of America, we have to ask
the tough questions regarding why a once proud, stable, mighty
country is now succumbing to shrill internecine battles over
matters that could be creatively and amicably resolved. Based
on an extensive examination of data and other cultural information, I'd like to offer a perspective for your consideration.

WORLDVIEWS AND VALUES

Everyone has some type of religious faith. That faith shapes our
worldviews. Those worldviews dictate the values we embrace.
These values influence the choices we make and the lives we
lead.

The United States is a land in which there are competing worldviews and values, which produce diverse lifestyles and expectations. The breadth of worldviews and values that reside within the

nation are partly responsible for the variety that has enabled the country to continue to play a major role on the world stage.

But that variety can sometimes create a gulf between what makes for a strong and cohesive nation and one that is satisfied simply to feel good in the moment. America is faced with this dilemma today: should we demonstrate restraint and invest in cross-tribal relationships in order to remain a strong and vibrant nation over the long run, or should we give in to our desire to take the road that demands less now but will likely lead to our demise in the future?

Human history shows that sometimes we forget that what is possible and what is fruitful are two different things. America appears to be at a juncture in history where we have to clarify the shared values that are advantageous and the divergent viewpoints that could ultimately harm the nation.

A WORD ABOUT THE RESEARCH

This book addresses what some of my friends have characterized as a "big idea." I want you to know that it is not simply a thought that has germinated in my mind for a while before I decided to commit it to paper. The concepts presented in these pages were borne from more than one million dollars' worth of research.

For the past quarter century, I have been studying the role of faith in American society. From the nationwide surveys investigating people's faith that my company regularly conducts with representative samples of one thousand or more adults, I have developed an extensive sense of what makes Americans tick. Each of our surveys includes a standard battery of theolographic questions—inquiries regarding what they believe, how they practice their faith, the role of faith, how it becomes integrated into their daily experience, and so forth.

For this book, I combined the results from a number of surveys, using the common theolographic questions as the foundation through which to filter a very wide range of attitudes, behaviors, values, and perceptions expressed in the various surveys. In total, I had the opportunity to slice and dice the population in relation to more than 500 different measurement criteria (576 distinct variables, to be exact). Using various statistical techniques, I found that Americans' faith can be categorized into a series of segments, which we will refer to as the seven tribes. And it is on the basis of the information related to each tribe that I will be describing what is happening in our society today. **Please note that this is not a book of personal opinions but a compilation of thousands of opinions culled from the people being profiled.** I realize that not every member of any tribe thinks or behaves in exactly the same way. However, by providing an overview of each faith group, I believe we can come to a better understanding of what unites us. (For more information about the procedures used, read appendix 4, which describes our research methodology.)

ROAD MAP

Having made the argument that America is on a crash course for self-destruction, we can either sit back and watch, complicit in the collapse, or we can strategically attempt to revitalize the nation. Toward the latter course of action, let's take a strategic journey into the following areas.

Stage one

Identify and study the faith tribes: who they are, what they believe, how they live, and what they are passionate about. From this exploration we will be able to better identify and understand the core values that drive the nation—and may serve as the route to a better future.

Stage two

Identify and examine the prevalent worldviews that America's faith tribes embrace and determine what each body of beliefs and convictions adds to the American condition. Given our philosophical leanings, we can then identify common values and principles that satisfy the views of the seven tribes. Acknowledging and pursuing those shared values can facilitate the healing and restoration of our nation. The necessary dialogue that must occur could revolve around our shared commitment to these ideals.

Stage three
Explore the reasons behind the failure of American leaders and institutions—political, religious, and family—to unite the nation around a set of shared values and goals. Consider why they've been unable to maintain a healthy and robust dialogue around the critical dimensions of modern life. Beyond such analysis, though, we will consider action steps that each of those critical entities could take to move America toward restoration.

Stage four
Americans are fighting wars on many fronts: financial, moral, religious, educational, military, familial, and so forth. We will end this journey with a challenge to adopt a common view of where we, as a nation, can go in unison. Accepting and mastering the challenge will then allow us to become better world citizens. The United States will face continued crises and challenges, but if the people of this republic can learn to share a set of values and goals that resonate with our most deeply held convictions, we will be better equipped to handle the trials and exploit the opportunities that arise.

THERE IS NO TIME TO LOSE
Hundreds of once-great societies have risen and collapsed in the face of similar challenges. From history, we can learn how to sidestep the tribulations that led to their demise. It is a multifaceted challenge that requires everyone, not just our best and our brightest, to participate in the solution. Greatness never comes by the government or charismatic leaders coercing the people to get in line. Cultural endurance is not the result of endless

experimentation and self-indulgence. A satisfied citizenry does not emerge from being pampered and spared the hard work of investing in and sustaining democratic principles and practices.

If the United States is to enter its fourth century as a strong and enduring nation, it must embrace and embody the selfless values that carried the country through its first two-plus centuries of freedom and fulfillment. We are indeed a resilient nation, but if we insist on shedding communal sensibilities in favor of personal liberty and self-satisfaction, we will experience an agonizing demise. If, however, we remember that there is a greater good, indeed a higher calling, that we can collectively achieve, we can effectively contribute to making our nation and the entire world a better place.

Faith, shared values, compassionate and empathetic dialogue, visionary leadership, healthy families—these are the components of restoration that must be harnessed for the common good. We have the capacity. Will we use it?

CHAPTER
TWO
Casual Christians

THE FIRST faith tribe to understand is a group we will describe as the Casual Christians.[9] We start our analysis of America's family of faith tribes with this group because it is our only true megatribe. More than four out of every five adults in America consider themselves to be Christian. Most of the country's self-described Christians—80 percent of them, in fact—fit within the Casual Christian tribe. That means nearly two out of every three Americans are Casual Christians. In a nation of about 225 million adults, they are roughly 150 million of the total.

As you reflect on the profile of this group, you might be tempted to yawn with profound indifference, convinced that there is little to learn from a recitation of the attributes of a group that everyone knows so well. I encourage you, however, to pay attention to this profile, because it is the cornerstone around which seminal transformation in our society—and the current hemorrhaging of our nation—is taking place.

If you watch any of the crime investigation programs on television that have been popular in recent years, you may have noticed that the most important clues to solving crimes are not always lodged within hidden microscopic particles but sometimes are so obvious and accessible that we overlook them. In like manner, comprehending the real issues facing America requires us to uncover both the overt and covert factors that make our nation what it is today.

HOW CASUALS SEE THEMSELVES

Most Casuals are comfortable with themselves. They are likely to believe that they are making a positive difference in the world and adding value to it through their choices and actions. For the most part, they believe that other people see them as leaders, and they do what they can to promote their ideas and goals without stirring conflict or controversy: such friction makes them uncomfortable. In fact, they are not prone to taking risks and reject the label of social activist. Even though most leadership developers recognize that leadership, by definition, is about taking risks and stimulating some degree of conflict in order to bring about change, Casuals contend that they lead by maintaining stability and the status quo.

They perceive themselves to be independent thinkers and are conscious of their preference for having control over situations. Because they are skeptical about the motivations of other people, they prefer to dictate where things are going and how they will get there. Even though they are more likely than most to say they adapt easily to change and that they handle life's problems with aplomb, they are more likely to avoid change than to introduce it. They contend that they can be effective in their various life roles—such as parenting—without being change catalysts.

Casuals are tethered to a set of core values that dictate their behavior and attitudes, yet they remain very open to a wide array of moral perspectives and lifestyles. They do not consider this to be caving in to social pressure as much as satisfying their desire to get along with others and to experiment with new options. They claim to support "traditional family values," but are equally as prone to adopting nontraditional viewpoints in order to stay connected to other people and to remain at peace with their world.

Casuals are highly relational people and put personal bonds ahead of ideological convictions. Their penchant for loyalty and reliability overwhelms the need to be right at all costs. In fact, they would rather be known as friendly and upbeat than intelligent or always right. They will admit that they are committed to getting ahead in life—but not at the expense of important personal relationships or their core values.

Among their central tenets is the importance of faith, and they are generally comfortable with their spiritual condition. Most Casuals (59 percent) think of themselves as "deeply spiritual" and feel that God has accepted them as they are, for who they are. This contributes greatly to their sense of peace with the world. They have no particular passion about vocally representing God and His ways in the world. Casuals are more interested in living a simple, low-key life filled with happiness and fulfillment than pursuing faith-based truth and righteousness.

While this group is not especially fit—exercise is not among their joys in life, and their physical condition often reflects this oversight—they confidently and proudly view themselves as self-made, self-sufficient individuals.

LOOKING AT THEIR LIVES

Because personal comfort is such a major objective, Casuals develop personal goals designed to facilitate such a life. Those goals generally revolve around keeping peace with everyone: God, family, friends, neighbors, and coworkers. They worry about things that will put undue pressure on them, such as financial debt or marital strife. To minimize their anxieties in life, they generally sidestep conversations about controversial matters, including religion and politics. Their tendency is to offer encouraging words to those who are down and to look for the upside in every situation. They feel that sharing their sunny outlook on life is one of the best gifts they can offer to others.

Most of the Casuals' lifestyle characteristics constitute the norm in America, which is not surprising given their massive numbers. For instance, their levels of ownership of a dozen types of technology are the same as the national average. The way they use the Internet corresponds to the national norm. How often they watch movies, the basis on which they select films to watch, and the particular movies they view mirror U.S. averages. Even their participation in activities like smoking, getting drunk, committing adultery, viewing pornography, buying lottery tickets, visiting psychics, and gossiping is indistinguishable from the nationwide averages. Their level of household debt is average, the prevalence of their engagement in culture-changing efforts such as boycotts and writing protest or complaint letters is average, and their favorite genres of movies and television programs are the same as everyone else's.

Average, average, average.

Perhaps because of their view of God as a benign and forgiving deity, Casuals do not get too excited about matters of faith. They are less likely than other Americans to look forward to going to church services, reading the Bible, or discussing their religious beliefs with others. In fact, they have relatively low levels of confidence in the clergy and have little desire to invest themselves in their faith communities. Their spiritual lives are not much of a priority.

And while they are somewhat ambivalent about moral standards, willing to alter their personal views to conform to the public will, they do harbor concerns that too much altering of moral and ethical norms could create future problems. That does not stop them, however, from considering various behaviors usually identified as immoral from a biblical perspective to be morally acceptable. Examples include cohabitation, gambling, and entertaining sexual fantasies that do not include one's spouse. Similarly, Casuals are not likely to change a television program they are watching simply because it contains morally questionable content or messages. Overall, this group pushes the boundaries of traditional Christian morality.

This same desire for comfort leads most Casuals to take action that enables them to be viewed as good people—largely in consideration of their images. But they are less driven to do such good deeds because of a compulsion to influence the lives of other people, to leave their marks upon the world, or to make a real difference in life. Fame is not on their to-do list. Establishing themselves as decent people who stay within the prescribed boundaries is more to their liking.

To their credit, however, they do have a soft spot in their hearts for the poor. They view poverty as one of the most serious problems facing the United States and would like to see the government do more to assist the disadvantaged. While they are not likely to volunteer their time to help poor people rise above their struggles, they are more likely than most to donate money to organizations that help the poor.

Family is also a major issue for Casuals. When asked to identify their highest priority in life, they rank among the highest of all tribes in putting family matters on top. In fact, a majority choose family over other possibilities such as faith, career, friends, lifestyle, health, and wealth. Casuals are also the tribe most likely to assert that other family members have the dominant influence on their thinking and behavior. And eight out of ten say that one of their highest goals in life is to be married and avoid divorce. The only long-term goal that outranks that is having good health.

On the political front, Casuals tend to be middle-of-the-road in their views, with occasional leanings toward the left or right. They usually reflect sympathy for the defenseless, whether that constitutes the poor, immigrants, minorities, or children (through better child-care options, improved schools, and better parenting). They are also sympathetic to the environmental movement, as reflected in their well-honed recycling habits and desire to see stricter environmental policies enacted.

Their open-mindedness is seen in their willingness to vote for a Mormon or a Muslim. They view voting as a privilege and are fairly regular in voting in presidential elections.

Not likely ever to be confused with the more conservative evangelical segment of the Christian community, Casuals nevertheless voice consistent support for the presence of Christian symbols and messages in the public square. They support allowing the Ten Commandments to be posted in public buildings. They favor retaining the words "In God We Trust" on our currency. They back the inclusion of the "one nation under God" line in our Pledge of Allegiance. And they even argue for teaching creationism in science classes and believe that parental approval should be required for a minor who seeks an abortion.

However, they veer from the preferences of the religious right in their increasing support of rights for homosexuals and their desire to see marriage redefined to allow same-sex couples to marry.

Many of their political views are shaped by the fact that they do not believe that absolute moral truths exist. They believe that although truth exists, it always depends on the situation and can best be determined by those involved in the circumstances in question.

Despite the fact that Casuals consider themselves to be Christian, almost universally own one or more Bibles, and consider the Bible to be God's words and principles for humankind to live by, less than 2 percent of them have a biblical worldview.[10] In other words, only a handful of Casuals respond to everyday situations largely on the basis of what they believe the Bible teaches in reference to those opportunities.

Our research also confirmed that this perspective on reality is passed on to the children of Casuals. While these parents are committed to bringing their children to church services and classes on a regular basis, very few teach their offspring that absolute moral truth exists or that faith should be a top priority in their lives.

PROFILING THEIR RELIGIOUS BELIEFS

The beliefs embraced by Casuals are an odd amalgam of biblical and extrabiblical views. But it is the combination of contrasting perspectives that fosters their lukewarm relationship with the Christian faith. In many instances, we find that Casuals seem to accept authentic biblical tenets, only to take contradictory positions when asked related theological questions.

Most Casuals (74 percent) say they are personally committed to Jesus Christ, and a similar proportion believe that God is the all-knowing, all-powerful Creator of the universe who still rules that universe today. They generally believe that their religious faith is an important component of who they are, and about two-thirds of them contend that the ultimate purpose of life is to love God with all their hearts, minds, strength, and souls—as commanded by Jesus Himself (see Luke 10:27). They attribute omnipotence to God, believing He knows the future, is the source of all power and authority, and is still involved in the world. And two-thirds of them concur that Jesus Christ is alive today.

But Casuals have an arm's-length relationship with their acknowledged Creator. Perhaps that is attributable to their apparent difficulty in relating to invisible, intangible spirits. After all, most of them do not believe that Satan or the Holy Spirit exists, and they are not sure what to make of the concepts of angels and demons. A major portion of Casuals believe that Jesus is God but that He sinned while on earth. That, of course, is a contradiction from biblical teaching, but it's reasonable since most Casuals believe the Bible is God's Word but that it contains some errors and is not to be taken literally. They seek to glean key principles without embracing the literal truth of its contents.

That very perspective—that mystically guided by God and relying heavily upon their own skills and abilities, they must make sense out of the world—is perhaps the foundational spiritual reality that defines Casuals. For instance, a large majority (more than two-thirds) believe that "God helps those who help themselves," which is a popular notion but not particularly biblical. Two-thirds of the Casuals believe that we have free will and can therefore chart our own courses to meaning, purpose, and success in life. In fact, less than one out of every three Casuals agree that success is about obedience to God rather than personal accomplishments in life.

Self-reliance is a big deal among Casuals. For instance, they firmly believe that people choose to be good or bad. The traditional Christian contention that we are born sinners and must seek God's strength through the forgiveness and presence of Jesus Christ in order to overcome our sin nature is a tough sell to this group. Further illuminating their path is the notion that God's highest desire for them is that they be happy. Casuals are twice as likely to believe that God wants them to achieve happiness as those who believe that He wants them to achieve holiness.

This independent streak helps explain why so many of the millions who claim to have a personal commitment to God through Christ are still uncertain about what will happen after they die: it's not something that they can control, and the Bible's teachings about salvation through grace simply do not resonate with them. Less than two out of every five Casuals (38 percent) believe they will have eternal life because of their own confession of sins and acceptance of Jesus Christ as their Savior, their only hope of receiving God's grace.

That same independent streak might also explain why Casuals generally have a low view of the importance of belonging to a genuine community of believers. They are happy to attend a church and perhaps even become a member, but they are notably less likely than others to seek attachment to an assembly of like-minded faithful. Toward that end, less than one out of every five (18 percent) believe that spiritual maturity requires a commitment to a particular community of faith and investing themselves in those relationships. I suspect that the massive amount of church shopping, hopping, and swapping is largely attributable to the Casuals—people for whom longevity in a family of faith is much less meaningful and attainable than investing in their biological families.

Casuals seem comfortable picking and choosing the princi- ples from the Bible that they believe are literally accurate. For instance, it is surprising to see their acceptance of so many of the miraculous events contained in the Scriptures. Four out of five believe that Jesus Christ was resurrected and was born to a virgin (Mary). Three out of four believe that Jesus did feed five thousand people with just a few loaves and fish and that He turned water into wine at the wedding in Cana. Roughly two- thirds of them accept at face value the stories of Moses dividing the Red Sea, Peter walking on the water with Jesus, Daniel sur- viving his time in the lions' den, David slaying Goliath, and the world being created in six days. Six out of ten believe the story of Adam and Eve in the Garden of Eden. Only about half accept the story of Samson losing his strength when Delilah facilitated his haircut.

Even so, what Casuals resonate with most in these stories is not so much the implications for their own lives and relation- ships with God as their pride at being associated with such a deity and the encouragement they draw from those narratives. Not much of it translates into a real relationship with the God they contend is living, nor does it motivate them to full devo- tion to a life centered on God. Casuals memorize very little in the Bible—just as they rarely memorize lines out of other great historical books. They esteem the Bible, but it is not their guidebook for life. Their relative ambivalence about the Bible is reflected in the fact that more than half of them don't even know what Bible translation they own and read most often.

The Christianity of the Casuals is a comfortable safety net for life. They see life as their personal responsibility, with God waiting in the wings to nudge them when necessary and to save them when times get truly desperate. Religion is a private mat- ter in their eyes, not something to be constantly talked about or aggressively shared with those whose lives have no direct connection with God. They read the Bible for solace more than instruction, and they take pleasure in its culturally accepted principles rather than admonition from its higher expectations of how to live. They believe that heaven and hell exist, and they feel that the ultimate destination of their souls rests in their hands: if they are good people and do enough good deeds over the course of their lifetimes, the God they believe exists will appreciate their good natures and reward them with eternity in heaven. Consequently, Christianity is not a real belief as much as another goal to pursue, along with happiness, success, and comfort.

HOW CASUALS PRACTICE THEIR FAITH

As their name implies, Casual Christians are rather laid-back about their faith practices. Most of them have one or two religious behaviors that they strive to practice consistently. For most, that includes prayer and maybe attending church services or taking a quick read from the Bible during the week. They often supplement these endeavors with a brief dose of Christian media: Christian radio (talk shows more than preaching programs), some Christian music (middle-of-the-road pop fare is most common), or a few minutes of Christian television (tuned in, surprisingly often, while they are preparing to go to church).

To put this in perspective, realize that less than one out of every five Casuals (18 percent) engage in all of the "big three" Christian practices in a typical week: attending a church service, reading the Bible, and praying.

Other, more intimate religious practices are similarly rare among Casuals. Experiencing times of personal, daily worship; intentionally pursuing new faith insights each day; purposefully seeking to help other people each day as a tribute to their love of God; spending time in silent prayer and meditation each day; and having daily discussions with other trusted believers to hold themselves accountable for practicing their faith are not likely to make the agenda of the overwhelming majority of Casuals. Our surveys show that although they see the potential value of such habits, they simply have not sufficiently prioritized these endeavors to incorporate them into their lives.

In fact, while Casuals devote themselves to success and achievement in life, and commonly set specific goals they strive to reach, they do not stretch that same practice into their faith life. Only a small percentage can identify any faith goals beyond "attending church more often" or vague ideals such as "being a better person."

Some people say that if you want to know the state of people's hearts, you should evaluate what they spend their money on. In this case, we find that most Casuals do contribute money to a church, and a majority supplement that giving by making donations to one or more other nonprofit organizations during the year. However, they give away an average of just five hundred dollars per year to all churches and nonprofits. And even though the concept of tithing—giving away 10 percent or more of one's income to the church or other nonprofits—is debated in Christian circles as to its modern-day relevance (many say that Jesus died to free us from such legalistic standards, liberating us to give as much as we can in order to advance God's ways)—less than 5 percent of the Casuals tithe their incomes. They donate an average of about 1.5 percent of their gross annual household incomes to churches and charities.

THE LONG VIEW

It is safe to say that Casual Christians have done what they can to accommodate Christianity within the framework of their personal goals and desires. Because they are actively seeking a pleasant and comfortable life, they concentrate on those elements of the Christian faith that fit within those parameters. Rather than allowing the Christian faith to shape their minds and hearts, they have chosen to fit Christianity within the box they have created for it. The outcome is a warm, fuzzy feeling about their faith of choice because it has been redefined according to their needs. Lacking belief in absolute moral standards, they feel no compulsion to challenge the country to pursue a different moral course. Despite their stated discomfort with the current moral condition and direction of the nation, their proposed solution is for people to adopt greater tolerance.

Casuals are fervently pursuing the American dream, with particular emphasis on liberty and happiness. They accept responsibility for making that dream a reality, resulting in the highest levels of stress and busyness admitted to by any of the seven tribes. Their beliefs and convictions change from time to time, based on their personal needs and expectations. This is facilitated by their ability to compartmentalize their faith and juggle it alongside other decision-making inputs. While it might seem a bit strong to characterize Casuals as treating God with an "out of sight, out of mind" approach, their lack of intimacy with Him is one of the defining features of this tribe.

THREE
Captive Christians

AT JUST 16 percent of the total adult population, the group we will label Captive Christians is hardly an imposing mass. While that represents about 36 million adults—roughly the size of California's population—it certainly pales in comparison to the numbers of the Casuals (whose population exceeds that of all of Russia). But as we noted earlier, size is not always the determining factor when it comes to cultural influence, nor does it necessarily affect one's fulfillment in life.

This segment of Christians most closely resembles what the media would probably refer to as evangelicals. However, Barna Group studies indicate that evangelicals are only half as numerous as Captives: based on the theological criteria (rather than self-report) approach we use, evangelicals are roughly 8 percent of the adult public.[11] There is substantial overlap between these two groups: seven out of every ten evangelicals qualify for the Captive category, and evangelicals comprise one-third of all the Captives in the nation. So while there is some similarity between the two classifications, evangelicals and Captives are not one and the same by any stretch.

The name Captive Christians stems from the fact that they are, as the apostle Paul described himself, voluntary slaves to Jesus Christ.[12] Their hearts have been so arrested by the love and grace of Christ that they are wholly captive to the mind and heart of God. Based on our extensive research, we find that the Captives are qualified to be known as followers of Christ. Their combination of Bible-based convictions and spiritual practices has transformed them into a different type of people. They are not carbon copies of Christ, but they are readily distinguishable from the more lax, cultural form of Christianity seen in the lives of the Casual Christians. They have successfully (although not perfectly) blended biblical beliefs, spiritual behavior, and their lifestyles into an integrated way of being.

The distinction between these two forms of Christianity is acknowledged in the Bible. In the second and third chapters of Revelation, Jesus describes the seven churches of Asia (now western Turkey). All seven claim to be Christian. But five of those communities of faith clearly disappointed God, and just two are praised for their commitment to His ways.

The criticisms of the churches that fell short are a stinging reprimand. Their faults include failing to prioritize God, lacking love, not consistently serving people, embracing unbiblical teaching and sexual immorality, being spiritually lukewarm, focusing on material comfort, compromising truth, tolerating sin and immorality, and possessing a superficial faith. By their own admission, Casual Christians are often characterized by many of these same attributes. While those characteristics are widely accepted in today's culture, they fall short of the standards set forth in the Bible.

The churches of Smyrna and Philadelphia are praised for honoring God and displaying a diligent faithfulness to God in all situations. They are described as being faithful advocates of God; obedient to His commands and principles and willing to persevere despite being harshly persecuted; materially impoverished; and outnumbered—characteristics that parallel some of the more striking qualities of Captive Christians. This tribe exhibits the soft heart required to demonstrate genuine Christian love in the midst of hardships. But Captives also mirror the unshakable determination evident within the churches of Smyrna and

Philadelphia. They recognize that this life is merely a battle-ground between the forces of good and evil, that everyone chooses a side, and that what we do on earth affects the lives of others in the present and for eternity.

Captives are more infatuated with the ways and ends of the supernatural dimension than they are with those of the contemporary material world. The supernatural may be invisible, but to the Captives it is very real and approachable. They are convinced that supernatural activity impacts the natural world every moment of every day. In this sense, Captives honor the past, accept the present, but live for the future, believing that today's troubles simply prepare them for coming trials—and for their eternal reward. The truths and principles that define a future that only God knows and controls radically affect how they live in the present. For most Americans, the unseen, super-natural world is unknowable, weird, and a bit scary—if they even believe that such a dimension exists. For Captive Christians, even though the supernatural dimension is neither fully dis-closed nor completely understood, it is their comfort zone.

Who are these otherworldly-minded people? Let's find out.

HOW CAPTIVES SEE THEMSELVES AND THE WORLD

When Captive Christians look in the mirror, they see spiritual beings, first and foremost, currently functioning in earthly bod-ies. They believe their lives are to be lived in the flesh, but for spiritual purposes and on the basis of biblical principles. They acknowledge that they are human—but also that they are innately spiritual. In their minds, spending time on earth in their physical bodies is simply a temporary and necessary phase they must experience before moving on to a more permanent and satisfying existence.

In bold contrast to the self-image of other tribes, Captives think of themselves as deeply spiritual creatures who are full-time servants of the living God of Abraham, Moses, David,

Peter, and Paul. They are not just churchgoers. These are people who see themselves as spiritual warriors gratefully possessing a vibrant relationship with God. As they think about what dimension of their lives is most highly developed, hands down they say it is the spiritual. They feel close to God and directed by the Holy Spirit, whom they believe literally lives within them. They are compelled by their love for God to do things that bring Him pleasure and glory.

Captives make no bones about it: they proudly proclaim that their lives have been significantly transformed by their faith in God, through a personal, hope-restoring relationship with His Son, Jesus Christ. That connection with God has moved them from walking through the paces on earth to voluntarily submitting to what they perceive to be His will for their lives. They possess a dogged commitment to fulfill that will.

While most Americans are skeptical of other people, Captives lack that wariness because they see people through a spiritual lens. They believe they have been called by God to live in this era of history to make a difference for His Kingdom, and that means loving other people. For the most part, they are mentally and emotionally committed to doing whatever they can to fulfill that calling.

Their lives are more low-key than the media might lead you to believe. They have the lowest level of stress of any of the faith tribes, an advantage they would attribute to their trust in God and their determination to live one day at a time. Their schedules tend to be less packed with activity, an oddity they attribute to their view of success as obeying God rather than achieving worldly success. Not surprisingly, then, they are also less likely than people from any other tribe to view themselves as "self-sufficient" and are more likely to claim that they are wholly dependent upon their God.

The result? More than any other tribe, Captives describe themselves as being "at peace" and "filled with joy." They also rate at the top of the scale on happiness.

Although their household incomes rank right in the middle of the seven tribes, Captives are most likely to say they are financially comfortable. They seem willing to live within their means and to moderate their desires. Various measures suggest they tend to be satisfied with what they have rather than pining for what they don't have. Captive Christians are not consummate consumers.

LIVING THE GOOD LIFE

Perhaps Captive Christians are comparatively comfortable with life because they appreciate consistent deep sleep. The research revealed that among all the things they look forward to, getting a good night's sleep at the end of the day was at the upper end of their "very desirable" list, far surpassing other popular activities such as watching television, traveling for pleasure, eating out, and exercising. In fact, the only thing that Captives look forward to more than a restful night is going to church! Other experiences they greatly look forward to include reading the Bible and spending time with family and friends.

When examining their major goals in life, the extensive faith commitment of members of this tribe is inescapable. Their ideal lives include being active in their churches, being close to God, and living out a deep commitment to Christianity. They want their lives to make a difference in the world, are dedicated to pursuing a clear purpose in life, are intent upon demonstrating the highest levels of integrity, long to live near their extended families, don't feel complete without good groups of close friends, and pledge to stay married to their first spouses. To facilitate these desires, they also hope to have excellent health.

Overall, their highest priorities revolve around two key elements: faith and family. Focusing on being the people that God made them to be and loving their families as much as possible makes it easier for them to eschew many of the lifestyle options that motivate their fellow Americans. For instance, Captives are lowest among all the tribes in terms of desiring comfortable lifestyles, high-paying jobs, large houses, and fame. They simply have a different set of desires than most other Americans, and their underlying motivations are drawn from their spiritual core.

Captives are perhaps the most consistent exemplars of old-style morality. Among all of the tribes, they are least likely to view pornography, get drunk, gamble, use profanity in public, gossip, use tobacco products, or commit adultery. They are the tribe that is most likely to serve the homeless, help the poor, discuss moral issues with other people, go out of their way to give words of encouragement to someone who is down, and pray for the needy.

To their credit, Captive Christians do not just talk the game, they walk it. After all, that's what makes them "captive." For instance, they have a tendency to back up their words and beliefs with cash: they donate the most money to the poor (71 percent above the per capita national average), and they spend the least on gambling (an average of twenty-six dollars annually, which is one-seventh the national average—and is spent mostly on lottery tickets).

Captives emerged as the tribe with the lowest levels of debt—and the highest levels of generosity. They almost universally give away money, and they do so with abandon: Captives donate an average of six dollars to nonprofit entities for every one dollar donated by a typical adult. In relation to church giving, they surpass the national norm by a ten-to-one ratio!

Even their attitudes about giving are different. While they are realistic about how much change one individual can produce in regard to poverty, they are the most vehement opponents of the idea that a situation is hopeless or that one person is powerless to alter the state of poverty, either domestically or globally. The deep-rooted faith of Captive Christians drives them to believe and behave differently in relation to human pain and suffering.

Their attitudes about other social drivers also deviate from the norm. A prime example is their wariness and distrust of the mass media. Captives see the media's impact on lives all around them and fear that little good is coming of it. For instance, as they look at their own lives, they believe that the greatest influence on their marriages and families—to their own horror—is media content, even though three-quarters of them also believe that their faith should have the greatest influence. Such challenges are seen as part of the spiritual and moral battle they are up against.

Their response to media dominance is unlike that of most of the tribes. For starters, they have the lowest level of exposure to media content across the board. Similarly, they are the tribe most likely to limit the amount of media exposure their children receive. In addition, if a movie or TV program they are watching contains immoral or inappropriate content, their default response is to interrupt it in favor of an alternative. And they are steadfastly opposed to allowing media—television and music in particular—to use the *F* word at will. They believe that advisory labels on product packaging do not go far enough to protect the public.

Such media concerns haunt Captives because they are especially sensitive to the power of media on the minds and hearts of children. Most of the tribes collaborate with the culture to create a seamless values-development experience for their children. Captives, in contrast, fear and resist the unconscious indoctrination of their youngsters into the prevailing mores of what they deem to be an increasingly decadent society. In response, nearly three-quarters of them (71 percent) teach their children a cluster of absolute moral truths that they believe are foundational to good decision making.[13] Uniquely, they contend that there are three critical factors that parents must deploy in consistent doses if they hope to raise stellar children: love, faith, and patience. In fact, this is the only tribe that considers the provision of a strong faith experience to be the most important contribution that parents can make to the lives of their children.

THE POLITICAL VANTAGE POINT

Interacting with these adults is very different than interacting with Casual Christians. When you query Captives about their view of the world and what it needs, their replies are invariably and primarily spiritual in nature. For instance, when asked to identify the most serious problems facing the nation, their most common answers relate to the moral and spiritual needs of the country. They overwhelmingly contend that the United States needs to improve the spiritual condition of its citizenry, upgrade the health of its churches, and radically alter the moral environment (especially in terms of media content). Quiz them about their goals in life, and they'll tell you they aspire to become more active in their faith community and to live in ways that influence people to know and obey God more completely. They are devoted to making the world a better place, but they believe that can happen only if spirituality is at the root of the solutions they bring to the table.

Not surprisingly, Captives are what political analysts would describe as "consistently conservative." Their views line up with what media label "the religious hard right." A mere 6 percent of them claim to be liberal. They favor an amendment to the Constitution banning gay marriage and defining marriage as a relationship strictly between a man and a woman. They strongly favor teaching creationism in public schools. They identify homosexual lifestyles and inappropriate (i.e., immoral) media content as pressing domestic issues. They strongly support retaining a Christian heritage in every vestige of public life: religious symbols on public buildings, posting the Ten Commandments in courts and government centers, and keeping phrases such as "In God We Trust" on money and "one nation under God" in the Pledge of Allegiance. They see abortion as a continuing plague on society that must be stopped.

These views are, of course, an outgrowth of their spiritual foundations. More than any other group, they contend that absolute moral truths exist and that such truths are clearly delineated in the Bible. As such, this group is the most likely to characterize cohabitation, gambling, and having sexual fantasies about someone to whom they are not married as immoral. And they overwhelmingly consider adultery, gay sex, pornography, abortion, and drunkenness to be immoral behaviors. There is little ambiguity in the moral perspectives of Captive Christians. Their firm convictions on these matters explain why they are the tribe that most frequently speaks with other people about matters of morality and faith.

Befitting their conservative posture, Captives are the tribe least likely to support government intervention in poverty, opting instead for family- and church-based solutions. And they are consistently unconvinced about the severity of environmental issues such as global warming and environmental protection.

Their conservative bona fides are highlighted by their voting patterns in previous presidential elections. A majority voted for Bob Dole in 1996. Two-thirds voted for George W. Bush in 2000, and a similar percentage voted for him in 2004. Without such solid backing from the Captives, Mr. Bush would not have won either victory.

The presidency is a matter of considerable concern to Captives. They are the group most likely to pray for the chief executive. They are the tribe most desirous of having a leader in the White House who has a firm commitment to his faith as well as a strong marriage and family life. Most would refuse to vote for a candidate seeking the presidency who was an atheist or agnostic (77 percent) or a Muslim (54 percent).

RELIGIOUS BELIEFS ARE CENTRAL

As you would probably expect, Captive Christians are the tribe that most closely tries to understand and follow biblical teachings. They revere the Bible and think of it as their handbook for life. Nine out of ten strongly believe that the Bible is accurate in all of the principles it teaches. Nine out of ten contend that the Bible is the Word of God, although they are pretty evenly divided between those who say it is to be taken literally and those who say it is accurate but contains some symbolic narratives. More than nine out of ten (94 percent) say the Bible is the only thing we need to know how to lead a meaningful life. Nine out of ten argue that the original manuscripts of the Bible were totally true and reliable. Nine out of ten believe that the Bible is trustworthy. They passionately reject the notion that the Bible is essentially the same as the sacred books of other faiths (e.g., the Koran, Book of Mormon, Bhagavad Gita, etc.) or that it teaches the same basic principles despite using different characters or stories. Perhaps the greatest confirmation of their trust and respect for the Bible is the fact that every one of the Captive Christians we interviewed—and there were more than five thousand of them—reads the Bible on his or her own (not just at church events) during the course of a typical week.

The perspectives they draw from the pages of the Scriptures generally reflect a conservative theological view—and one that distances them from most Americans, including the Casual Christians. They are far more likely than any other tribe to believe that Satan is real, the Holy Spirit exists, and Jesus lived a sinless life on earth. They believe that Jesus had a physical resurrection, not simply a spiritual one, and that He is alive today. (Every one of the Captives we interviewed took the Resurrection story literally.) And they typically accept the miracles described in the Scriptures at face value: 92 percent or more of the Captives take literally the stories of Moses parting the Red Sea, Peter walking on water with Jesus, Daniel surviving the lions' den, David defeating Goliath, the Virgin Birth, Jesus feeding the multitudes, Noah and the ark, and Jesus converting water into wine at the wedding. This is the tribe that most forcefully promotes the notion of a six-day creation process (86 percent adopt this view).

This segment is highly unified in its ideas about God. They universally believe that God is alive today, that He is the omnipotent and omniscient Creator of the universe who rules our world today and remains active in its proceedings. They contend that He knows everything about the future and that He is the source of all power and authority: nobody has influence unless God allows him or her to have it. Because the God of Israel is perfect, they posit, He is the standard for morality and the only entity qualified to judge people. Captives believe that God has outlined His moral expectations in the Bible, and so they rely on the Bible, more than anything or anyone else, to shape their moral convictions and choices.

To the Captive's mind, all evidence points to God: they see Him as the divine orchestrator of all things, giving people free will but remaining intimately involved in the life of every person. Almost all of them (96 percent) strongly believe that the purpose of life is to love God with all their hearts, minds, strength, and souls. They adamantly hold that several other tribes offend God by suggesting that He is the same as their god or gods.

All of the Captives are born-again Christians—that is, they say they have made a personal commitment to Jesus Christ that is important in their life, and they believe they will have eternal life only because they have confessed their sins to God and asked Jesus Christ to save them. A huge majority of the tribal members believe that salvation can only be a gift from God, something that cannot be earned by doing good deeds or by trying hard to be a good person. More than any other tribe, they believe that sin remains a relevant concept today, and that it has devastating effects on our lives.

This tribe is not just universally "absolutely committed" to Christianity. They strenuously maintain that other faiths do not worship the same God and that everyone's sole hope for salvation lies in a grace-based relationship with the God of Israel. They deeply believe that a person cannot live a meaningful or satisfying life apart from their God. They say that Christianity is significantly different from other faiths in its principles, teachings, and expectations. When challenged about the apparent exclusivity of their views, they respond that these are God's rules, not theirs; that the Christian faith is available and accessible to all who seek to know and bond with God; and that God Himself invites and desires all people to establish lifesaving, fulfilling relationships with Him.

But make no mistake about it, theirs is a faith with unwavering standards. The Bible establishes the standards of obedience, they maintain, and there are positive or negative consequences for each of our choices. They submit that human beings are in the midst of a fierce spiritual war for their souls, and that both God and His enemy Satan are vying for our attention and allegiance. Captives would generally admit that God has thus far allowed Satan to win many battles in this war on the earth, based on the decaying moral behavior of Americans, but that God will emerge victorious at the end of time. God grants everyone the ability to make his or her own moral and spiritual choices, including eternal destiny, based on His parameters.

With these beliefs in mind, then, it is not surprising that this tribe stands out as the one in which its members say their most important relationship in life is with God; their most important reference group is their church; the most important decision they have ever made was when they repented and accepted Jesus Christ as Savior; and that the thing that has the greatest influence on their values and important life decisions is the Bible.

FAITH IN PRACTICE

So what would you expect to find when you study the religious behaviors of the Captive Christians? Probably exactly what we discovered. They consistently attend church services. They read the Bible frequently and regularly, studying it for clues about how to lead a holier life. They are the most common participants in faith-education settings. One example is Sunday school classes: with 60 percent showing up in a typical week, they are nearly four times as likely to attend as are Casuals. Another example is involvement in a small group or Bible study group, which almost 60 percent attend in an average week, also four times the norm among Casuals.

But Captive Christians pursue their faith well beyond "the big show," as church worship services are sometimes called these days. They are far more likely than people from any other tribe to seek an intimate, personal worship experience with God every day (53 percent); to pray multiple times during the day; to have a "quiet time" each day during which they meditate on the content they have read in the Bible and allow God to impact them; and to look forward to discussing their religious perspectives with other people. They are the most loyal audience for Christian radio, religious TV, and Christian books. They also emerged as the tribe most likely to serve other people and to conscientiously seek to integrate their faith into every dimension of their lives.

Faith is always on their minds. Incorporating their principles into their behaviors is a challenge that dominates their daily experiences.

THE WHOLE PACKAGE

The interesting realization from surveying thousands of Captive Christians is that most of them possess a disarming humility about their faith. Even though they have devoted countless hours to putting their faith into practice, a large share of them would eagerly acknowledge that they have a long way to go before they are mature in that faith.

The belligerence that the media report as emblematic of such followers of Christ is often taken out of context. When Captive Christians critique the culture, they claim they are not demonstrating a holier-than-thou demeanor as much as a righteous anger that the God they love and serve is being offended by the nation's choices. As God's hands and feet on the earth, they feel compelled to present His case as earnestly and passionately as they can, for they are deeply in love with the God who created and saved them.

Many people might read the Captive profile and feel sorry for them. "They're so one-dimensional" or "they are too rigid to enjoy what their God created" are some of the reactions we've heard people from other tribes offer about the Captives. But their criticisms may be a misreading. Captive Christians are not one-note songs; in fact, they might respond to these judgments by saying that other tribes are simply tone-deaf. And they would say it with a deep concern for the souls and lives of their fellow humans, praying that God would be able to capture their minds and hearts in the same way that He won over their own.

Make no mistake about it: the intensity of their religious beliefs and the imprinting of their spiritual experiences have made the Captive Christians a tribe to be reckoned with. What they lack in numbers they make up for in passion and determination, based on their belief that what they do matters greatly to God and that His love for them compels them to respond in kind by seeking to influence the world for His glory. They take heart in the fact that the Bible provides story after story of God using a remnant of committed followers to do works far greater than their meager numbers should have produced. True to biblical admonitions, they fear no one but God.

For members of this tribe, faith is not just a weekend journey designed to give them some inspiration and comfort; faith is the very heart of their existence and daily purpose.

CHAPTER
FOUR
American Jews

AFTER more than twenty centuries of relative stability, the past century has introduced unprecedented upheaval and reconstruction into the lives of Jews around the world. Beginning in the latter part of the nineteenth century, massive numbers of Jewish people emigrated from Europe to North America. In the middle of the twentieth century, Adolf Hitler's forces exterminated more than six million Jews and instigated the flight of many others, significantly changing the profile of that community. Shortly thereafter, in 1948, the establishment of a Jewish homeland (i.e., the state of Israel) marked another milestone in Jewish history.

Those events represent rapid and prolific change in the life of the Jewish community. The world's largest Jewish population now resides in the United States—about 6.5 million people, representing close to half of all Jews on the planet. Contemporary Judaism has its roots in the ancient Middle East but its heart in the postmodern West.

The changes redefining Judaism are extensive. Beyond the relocation of the locus of gravity within the community, Jews have now adopted a new set of values derived from their North American center; a new language through which to communicate; and a freewheeling spiritual environment. Throughout their history, of course, Jews have certainly struggled, but they have shown an uncanny knack for adaptation over the years.

It has been suggested that a number of critical themes underly Jewish life. One of those is continuity: accepting the importance of their tribal traditions, customs, teachings, and relationships. A second theme is that of survival: sustaining a sense of community and heritage. The third theme is the insistence on authenticity: retaining a unique identity and viable presence in the midst of a spiritually competitive culture.

In addition, a fourth theme is triumph over oppression. Whether it was the hardships resulting from the harsh rule of Pharaoh in Egypt or the evil intent and breathtaking cruelty of Adolf Hitler and the Third Reich, the mere existence of Jews is a testimony to their capacity to withstand and overcome even the most despicable examples of man's inhumanity toward the human race.[14] It seems that Jews have juggled these themes with sufficient skill to forge a unique tribal identity in the United States.

Rabbi Arthur Blecher insightfully points out that Judaism is not so much a religion, as American Christians think of religions, as it is a civilization or culture.[15] In other words, being Jewish is more about belonging to a community than adhering to a faith system defined by beliefs and religious rituals. Indisputably, custom, tradition, and ceremony are central elements of the Jewish experience and life, but there is much less emphasis and consternation about theology and doctrine than is found in Christian circles. Jews are a rather tolerant lot when it comes to theology; they have a diverse set of beliefs. In some ways, this tribe is more of a community with a shared history and culture than a group connected by a shared doctrine. Rather than being a story about the influence of a narrowly defined, well-preserved series of spiritual truths, the common bond of the Jews is a reflection of their alienation from the mainstream, their dogged determination, and their geographic mobility.

Another important historical factor that defines Jewish life in America is that the community is divided into three main sects: Orthodox, Conservative, and Reform. Just as American

Protestantism has splintered into more than two hundred different denominations, so has Judaism fragmented (although much less dramatically) into three distinct branches. The major points of disagreement relate to their beliefs about God, the interpretation of their sacred writings, adherence to their law and traditions, and commitment to their community.

Jews make up only about 2 percent of the U.S. population. For a group of people so small in numbers, they have had an enormous influence on American society. Apart from the well-trafficked stereotypes, who are they?

WHO THEY THINK THEY ARE

While most Jewish people have only a general sense of their roots, they understand they are a people who have endured and triumphed over hardship. Their determination to gut it out and overcome—what some might call their chutzpah—is a testimony to their ancestors. American Jews have overcome many difficulties in their century (or less) on American soil: religious discrimination, numerical insignificance, and more. They are survivors, and even today they tend to see themselves in that way.

Befitting that background, Jews view themselves as tough. They relish a good argument; backing down from a disagreement is uncommon. The data indicate that members of this tribe are more comfortable with conflict than are people from any other tribe. It is not unusual for them to initiate conflict as a means of moving closer to their goals.

This mental toughness, however, takes a toll emotionally. Perhaps because they so often feel it is them against the world, they score the lowest of all the tribes on our survey measures regarding happiness, joy, and feeling at peace. But one gets the sense that many Jewish Americans also derive a degree of identity, strength, and motivation from the emotional discouragement that is second nature to them.

Part of the compensation for their emotional challenges may

come from their self-image as achievers. They are substantially more likely than most Americans to view themselves as leaders—and to believe that others see them as such. That helps to explain why they are more likely than others to consider themselves to be serious and focused and why they prefer to be in control.

If any evidence of their performance is required, the track record of Jews in American business is extraordinary: their rise to the upper echelons of influence and authority belies their numbers. They are 63 percent more likely than average to live in households in the top fifth of the income brackets. This is partially attributable to their dedication to education: they are 71 percent more likely than the U.S. norm to be college graduates. More than any other tribe, Jews have embraced education as the means to success and stability in this country. Given their socioeconomic prominence, it is not surprising that the research also reveals that Jews rate higher than do people from other tribes in terms of their willingness to take risks in life. They are a case study in support of the axiom "Nothing ventured, nothing gained."

Jewish people put a lot of stock in community. Their understanding of community, however, is quite different from that of Christians. They accept any Jew into their fold simply on the basis of their shared heritage. They see themselves as highly relational individuals, perhaps a reflection of the mobility and oral tradition that are hallmarks of the ancient Israelites.

Family is important to members of this tribe, but once again it is perceived differently than it is by Christians. Most Americans think of family as a connection based partly upon bloodlines and partly upon the adoption of shared values and rules. In Jewish circles, family is more about heritage than rules. Our research discovered that the existence of "traditional family values" is largely dismissed by Jews as a cultural contrivance, yet the bonds between parent and child, and between siblings, are stronger than those found in non-Jewish households. In a Jewish family, you cannot earn your standing—it is yours because you are a relative and you are Jewish, no matter how you think or behave. In that manner, family is a source of tremendous stability and strength for Jews.

HOW JEWS THINK AND LIVE

Jews make no bones about it: they neither live simple lives nor do they aspire to. Unlike Christians and Muslims, who view simplicity as virtuous, Jewish Americans work hard and want the toys and experiences that money can buy. They tend to be proud of their accomplishments and look forward to owning material goods and having experiences that are seen as part of the reward for their efforts. Prosperity is seen as a symbol of their ability to overcome the odds; it is the community's signal to the world that they are a small but mighty force. Surprisingly, despite their higher household incomes and other indicators of wealth, Jews are no more likely than anyone else in the United States to say they live comfortably, perhaps reflecting loftier lifestyle expectations.

Their life goals differ from those of other tribes. Their dominant desires are to be healthy and well-educated; have a tightly knit family and trustworthy friends; be known as people of integrity; and be aware of and well-informed about what is going on in the world. Interestingly, a slight majority of Jews (52 percent) say that half or more of their close friends are Jews, an indication of the awareness Jews maintain of those who share their heritage.[16]

Some goals that might have been expected—such as having a high-paying job, living in a large home, traveling the world for pleasure, or being located close to relatives—are only moderately important to this tribe.[17]

Life outcomes related to faith, such as having a close relationship with God or being active in their synagogues, are of keen interest to relatively few Jewish people. This is consistent with the fact that when asked to describe their highest priority in life, only 2 percent mentioned their faith—the lowest level among the tribes (tied with that of atheists and agnostics). The other category of life goal that ranks low on the scale is that pertaining to supporting or living in concert with traditional morals.

Overall, members of the Jewish tribe do not feel bound by traditional moral perspectives. Few of them (about one out of five) believe that absolute moral truth exists; they generally contend that truth is dependent upon circumstances and interpretation. Consequently, Jews are significantly less worried about the moral condition of the nation than are people from other Christian-related tribes (i.e., Captives, Casuals, and Mormons). They are highly unlikely to turn off television programs or avoid movies that contain R-rated or objectionable content. (The exception is violence: Members of this group are less prone to watch or enjoy media content that is packed with violence. This tendency may be related to their history as targets of violence.) Along with the Skeptics, they are among those least concerned about the moral issues related to pornography, profanity, homosexuality, gambling, adultery, abortion, and excessive drinking. By and large, Jewish adults argue that these are personal choices that individuals must make for themselves and then live with the consequences.

In the eyes of Jewish Americans, people are ethically and morally frail: they are prone to lying, stealing, cheating, and other corrupt acts. Jews generally accept this as part of the human condition: it is what it is. Rather than devote themselves to changing such tendencies as Captives do, Jews are more likely to adopt a more defensive posture by adjusting their lives in anticipation of such behavior. They do not see much value in laws or personal campaigns designed to alter the course of moral choices; they prefer to put those decisions in people's hands and simply deal with the results.

That is not to say, however, that Jews let such issues pass without comment. To the contrary, they enjoy discussing such matters. In fact, the survey data suggest that they enjoy talking about (and even debating) a wide range of topics. They are more likely than most other tribes to get involved in discussions about controversial matters such as morality and ethics, religious beliefs, government policies, finances, and parenting choices. (They are also more likely to engage in spirited dialogue about less controversial topics such as sports.) Given their mindset, the objective of such discussions is not necessarily to win people to their side, but to be sure they get a fair hearing—and an opportunity to make their own decisions and choices. Jews enjoy the verbal jousting; it is one of the favorite sports of this tribe.

The causes that get them excited—besides support for the state of Israel—are most likely to be those associated with social injustice. They are not likely to volunteer their time to such causes, but they are likely to provide verbal and financial support to the issues that move them. They are more likely than most Americans to get riled up about various forms of injustice, such as slavery, child exploitation, and poverty caused by the absence of opportunity. Once again, cognizant of their own history, these are the types of issues with which Jews have significant empathy. In addition, they are also more likely to be concerned about environmental issues, including global warming. Most say that they want to make a positive difference in the world; they simply choose their means of doing so carefully.

Another factor that bears mentioning is the challenge of interfaith marriages. Overall, one-third of all Jews who are married have chosen partners who are outside the Jewish faith. There is widespread concern that this is both weakening the faith of those Jews (and their children) involved in such marriages and that the replacement rate is below that which will enable Judaism to grow in America. The trend line is ominous: of the Jews married prior to 1970, just 13 percent were interfaith marriages. Among Jews married between 1996 and 2001, almost half (47 percent) were interfaith unions. The impact of these blended marriages is startling: 96 percent of the children raised by parents who are both Jews are raised to be Jewish compared to just 33 percent of the children who grow up in homes where only one parent is Jewish. Data regarding the religious choices of parents in interfaith homes also indicate that the Jews in those marriages abandon many of the core Jewish faith practices.[18]

POLITICS AND GOVERNMENT

Jews are notoriously liberal in their political leanings. Half are registered to vote as Democrats, and most of the rest are independent of a party affiliation. Although the Republican Party is widely perceived to support business and the wealthy—two characteristics that define the Jewish population—the political philosophy of Jews advocates an extensive role for government in promoting social justice and providing a wide range of services. Ideologically, Jews are slightly more than twice as likely as the national average to describe themselves as politically liberal and only half as likely as the norm to embrace the label "politically conservative."

Because of these positions, Jews are less likely than Christian-oriented tribes to favor government policies that place limitations on personal behavior (e.g., abortion, gay marriage) and upon the inclusion of any form of religious thinking in public life (e.g., having "In God We Trust" on currency, including "one nation under God" in the Pledge of Allegiance, or even teaching the creation model in schools). Jews are generally opposed to changes in public policy that would strengthen support for traditional marriage at the expense of alternative relationships.

Our data find that Jews are also reticent to beef up regulations regarding the moral content or standards for mass media. In fact, we have also found that they become disturbed by well-organized efforts (such as those by Captives) to push for a religious or Christian morality agenda in the public arena—even though most of those efforts are based on traditional Judeo-Christian values drawn from the Pentateuch (the first five books of the Old Testament, which are widely accepted as authoritative in Jewish circles).

Their voting patterns in recent presidential elections confirm their liberal, Democratic orientation. In the 2000 election, Jews preferred Al Gore to George W. Bush by a five-to-one margin. In 2004, they opted for John Kerry over George W. Bush by a three-to-one margin.

WHAT JEWS BELIEVE AND PRACTICE

Although they are sometimes referred to as "people of the Old Testament," survey data point out that most Jews in the United States do not relate to that characterization. They see themselves more as a society based on common history and cultural preferences than a cohesive faith-driven people group that accepts the teaching and parameters of an ancient holy book.

As noted earlier, Jews rarely view themselves as individuals defined by their religious beliefs. While half of all American Jews say their religious faith is very important to them, for many of those people the importance of Judaism lies in the cultural identity it provides, rather than the moral and spiritual guidance it establishes. In fact, only a minority (four out of ten) think of themselves as deeply spiritual, and a mere 2 percent say that their religious faith is their highest priority in life.

Putting that in perspective, just one-quarter of Jews (24 percent) claim that the primary purpose of their lives is to love God with all their hearts, strength, and souls—a command given to the Jewish people directly by God through Moses (Deuteronomy 6:5). In considering the basis for their worldview and decision making, a series of questions indicated that Jews are more likely to trust science, reason, and logic than ancient sacred documents or teachings based on faith. Relatively few Jews—about one out of every four—say they think about some aspect of their faith during a typical day.

There is no particular book or form of documentation that a

majority of Jews accept as holy writ. The closest are the Bible (embraced by four out of every ten as "sacred or holy literature") and the Torah (the first five books of the Bible, deemed to be holy or sacred by one out of every three Jews). Other books deemed holy by many Jewish scholars and rabbis, such as the Tanakh, Nevi'im, and the Talmud, are each held in similar esteem by less than one out of every twenty Jews.

Most Jews perceive the Bible with suspicion. The community is evenly divided between those who say the Bible is a work of men (46 percent) and those who believe it is the Word of God (48 percent). However, among those who say it is the Word of God, a majority contend that it is not to be taken literally since it contains many errors and human interpretations, even though it was inspired by God. Overall, just one out of every six Jews (17 percent) firmly believes that all of the principles taught in the Bible are an accurate representation of God's actual words and standards.

As a result, almost all of the miracles described in the Bible after its first five books (Genesis, Exodus, Leviticus, Numbers, and Deuteronomy) are rejected. Even a number of Old Testament stories, such as David defeating Goliath with a slingshot, Daniel surviving the lions in the den, and Samson's incredible acts of strength, are widely dismissed as allegorical. The New Testament stories about Jesus—being born of a virgin, turning water into wine, walking on water, feeding the crowds, and being resurrected from the dead—are also repudiated. Surprisingly, the story of God creating the universe is also generally discarded in favor of more modern (i.e., scientific) explanations. Other narratives from the Pentateuch, however—such as Moses splitting the Red Sea, Noah and the great Flood, Adam and Eve in the Garden of Eden—are more commonly adopted as legitimate depictions of historical events.

Every faith system has some elements that are nearly universally embraced by its adherents. Interestingly, a common perception about God is not such an element within the Jewish community. Only about one-third of Jews (36 percent) would describe God in ways consistent with teaching in the Pentateuch: omnipotent, omniscient, Creator of the universe, ruler of the world today. Another third (32 percent) embrace variations on Eastern views of deity: that God refers either to "the total realization of personal, human potential" or "represents a state of higher consciousness that a person may reach." The remaining third possess a variety of views (e.g., there are many gods, every human is a god, God does not exist, etc.).

That ambiguity about God bleeds into Jewish perspectives on salvation and eternal consequences. Overall, Jews do not believe that anyone can be certain as to what his or her eternal destiny will be. They tend to view redemption as a process, not an event or a gift from God. But more important, their views must be understood within the larger theological context.

Most American Jews believe that God—whatever or whoever that is—is not personally involved in people's lives. They understand that Presence to be distant and perhaps even disinterested in the details of their lives. That deity is also limited in the minds of most Jews. For instance, a slim majority believe that God does not know the future. A similar proportion say He does not perform miracles. And only one out of every five Jews believes that God created the universe. A much higher proportion side with scientists and philosophers who have developed alternative models based upon a combination of science and reason.

So when it comes to salvation, making sense of the possibilities is obfuscated by the general fuzziness about God, His expectations (since there is no sacred literature that Jews universally and literally accept), and the workings of the spiritual realm.

For instance, only half of Jews believe that people have souls that continue after the completion of their earthly existence. Only one out of every six (16 percent) claims that "success" is determined by obedience to God's commands, as laid out in the Bible. Most Jews accept the concept of sin, but because three-fourths of them reject the idea of absolute moral truths, identifying sin is difficult if not impossible. Even the notion of a supernatural enemy of God (Satan) is widely disputed among Jews: only one-fifth believe there is an evil spiritual being who is powerful and defies God. Likewise, most Jews dismiss the idea that there are other spiritual forces (e.g., demons) that can affect people's lives.

In the end, a large number of American Jews adopt the view that once people die, their entire existence is completed. Among those who believe there is something after life on earth, there are divergent assumptions ranging from traditional views of heaven and hell to more postmodern variations that are derived from cultural conversations more than Jewish tradition or teaching. Those who contend that there is an afterlife are most likely to say that assignment to the positive location (e.g., heaven) is dependent upon an unfathomable combination of God's mercy and how a person lived his or her life. That helps to explain why two-thirds of all Jews believe that "God helps those who help themselves." Jews are a self-reliant, can-do tribe.

As for their faith practices, American Jews are not overly observant. Only one-quarter of the tribe attend Jewish religious services at a synagogue or temple once a month or more. A slightly lower percentage attend some type of religious education classes or programs. Involvement in seasonal services or events runs high—three-quarters participate in a Passover seder, almost as many light Chanukah candles, and about six out of ten fast on Yom Kippur. But, in general, physical engagement in communal spiritual events is minimal.[19]

PUSHING THE BOUNDARIES OF FAITH
The research data certainly portray American Jews as very distant relatives of the Captives, even though they share a similar spiritual ancestry. Whereas a substantial slice of the Captive segment rejects Christianity as a religion (they see it as an organic relationship and a trust rather than a set of rituals and rules), Jews have championed that notion more fervently than the

Captives would feel comfortable with. On the other hand, Jews contend that the Captives have pushed the foundations of the Jewish faith into areas of life it was never intended to invade.

It is an irony of history and human progress that the foundations of our nation's moral boundaries, as reflected in our laws and policies, have been widely ignored or rejected by the tribe from which those boundaries were borrowed. To understand that shift, we have to remember that American Judaism prizes freedom of interpretation in relation to its sacred texts, enabling Jews in good conscience to arrive at moral and spiritual conclusions that stray from historic Jewish positions.

Some have also observed that when people have no belief in any kind of life after death, their behavior in this life has less significant consequences, providing them a greater sense of freedom to do whatever they desire. Absent any certainty that there is a personal and omnipotent God who will judge people for sin and who may choose to sentence them to some type of eternal (or perhaps temporary) punishment or banishment, these people are left with a WYSIWYG existence: what you see is what you get. Our research indicates that a majority of American Jews are placing their bets on WYSIWYG rather than WYPIWYG (i.e., what Yahweh promises is what you get).

It is also quite telling that there is a substantial gap between what rabbis of all three major Jewish sects teach and what the "Jews in the pews" believe and practice. This is similar to the chasm between what most Protestant pastors teach and what Casuals believe and do. In both cases, what the faith in question has morphed into bears little resemblance to the intended faith experience.

But if faith is meant to provide a transformation experience for its followers, American Judaism has a ways to go before it satisfies that objective. Today, only one out of four Jews in the United States (27 percent) says that his or her faith has been life transforming. The only tribe that has found its faith to have less impact on members' lives is the Skeptics—the people who have no religious faith at all.

CHAPTER
FIVE
The Mormon Expansion

THE CHURCH of Jesus Christ of Latter-day Saints—most commonly known as LDS or the Mormon church—is a rarity: a major faith group that was birthed in the United States. Judaism, Christianity, and Islam were imported from the Middle East, and the dominant strains of Pantheism have come from the Far East. The Mormon faith is rooted in elements of the Christian faith and began in 1830 with the publication of Joseph Smith's visions and revelations, which developed into the Book of Mormon. Under the leadership of Brigham Young, the group eventually moved to Utah and began an aggressive expansion that has produced more than 13 million members across the globe, about 5 million of whom are in the United States. They represent about 1.5 percent of the U.S. population.

Mormons are a controversial and confusing group within the American context. For instance, the LDS church vehemently argues that it is a Christian body, yet it does not accept many of the central Christian teachings and beliefs. It claims to be a Bible-believing church, yet it puts other documents (such as the Book of Mormon) and teachings on par with the Bible. It has a history of endorsing, if not promoting, polygamy, although its church laws have been changed to outlaw that practice. A significant share of the American public—about one-quarter—continue to believe that the Mormon church is a cult, not a true member of the Christian community. Indeed, questions about the beliefs and practices of Mormons helped undermine the presidential campaign of Governor Mitt Romney in the 2008 Republican primaries.

The aggressive evangelistic activity of the Mormon church sustains a high profile for that body. Our studies show that there is substantial turnover within Mormon ranks: tens of thousands join in any given year, and a similar number leave in any given year, generally producing a small net gain for the LDS church. Formerly located almost exclusively within Utah, Mormons are now spread throughout the nation (although about 40 percent of them live in Utah).

HOW MORMONS SEE THEMSELVES

As much as anything, Mormons think of themselves as family people. They are much more likely to marry than are any other tribe. They marry younger. Their marriages last longer. They have more children. When asked to identify their top priority in life, family is the overwhelming answer: three-fourths (77 percent) cite family, compared to just 8 percent who named success and a comfortable lifestyle and 5 percent who listed their faith. More than 97 percent of the Mormons we have interviewed said they strongly support "traditional family values." If a branding expert were to determine the most appropriate positioning of Mormons, the brand would undoubtedly hinge on the tribe's family emphasis.

The self-image of Mormons is not solely about family, though. The faith of this tribe's members is also front and center in how they see themselves. Nine out of ten Mormons say that their faith is very important in their life, ranking them a close second to the Captives on that measure. Similarly, three-quarters of all Mormon adults describe themselves as "full-time servants of God," once again second only to the Captives. Each is also far more likely than the average American to label himself or herself a "committed Christian" (80 percent do so, compared to 65 percent of all adults).

Mormons see themselves as very loyal and reliable people: more than 95 percent describe themselves that way, another carryover from their faith teachings. More than nine out of ten also claim to be happy, at peace with life, and able to effectively cope with the problems they encounter. Most of them feel they have a clear sense of the meaning and purpose of their lives; just one-quarter say they are still trying to answer such questions. That is about half the proportion found among the population at large.

One interesting outcome from the research is that Mormons possess the highest stress levels (along with Muslims) of any tribe. Whether that stems from the usual strains related to raising children, the difficulty of being associated with a faith group that struggles to achieve acceptance by mainstream culture, or other reasons is unclear.

Another element of their self-image is that of "social activist." Perhaps because they have had to fight for acceptance for so long, they are accustomed to standing up against the culture for the things they consider important. One out of every three Mormons believes he or she is a social activist, trailing only the Muslim tribe in that regard.

HOW MORMONS THINK AND LIVE

Four out of five Mormons say they live simple lives. While the survey data do not fully support that claim—for instance, they own just as many electronic and technological gadgets as the average American—some of the research findings do support this self-perception. The goals they have set for their lives place outcomes such as fame, owning the latest in electronic gadgets, having a large house, and traveling the world for pleasure toward the bottom of the list. They do not appear to be consummate consumers: their levels of household debt are below average.

Mormons are renowned for the "squeaky clean" lives they lead. The data confirm the accuracy of the image. Mormons are much less likely than any other tribe to get drunk, use profanity, gossip, download pornography on the Internet, engage in adultery, use tobacco products, gamble, or buy lottery tickets.

Of all seven tribes, Mormons are most aware of and concerned about the impact of media content on their thinking and behavior. Along with the Captives, they rank highest among the tribes when it comes to turning off immoral or inappropriate television programming. Not surprisingly, Mormons are not a prolific audience for soap operas and reality shows—in fact, they are among the least likely to view such programs. Interestingly, they are among the most likely audience for science fiction programming. And while they enjoy movies, they watch fewer films in theaters than do other tribes—but make up for that deficit by watching a much higher number in their homes via DVD. Doing so enables them both to monitor and control the content more carefully and to afford such viewing for their large families.

Morality in the media is just one aspect of values and lifestyle choices that concerns Mormons. Along with the Captives, they are almost universally troubled by the moral condition of the country: nine out of ten express grave concerns about the condition and direction of our moral standards. Few Mormons harbor confidence in the moral character of the nation's leaders, whether they are involved in business, government, religion, education, or the media. They generally fear that our nation is drifting in the wrong direction morally and ethically.

Such consternation reflects the worldview of Mormons. They are about 40 percent more likely than the norm to believe that absolute moral truth exists. Overall, a slight majority accepts the idea of absolute morality. Those people are evenly divided between saying such teaching is rooted in the Bible and seeing it as a perspective they gleaned from their church's teaching. The Captives are the only other tribe among which a majority adopt absolute moral truth as a reality.

To their credit, Mormons emerge as the tribe whose members are most likely to say they are interested in becoming better people. That same mind-set is reflected in their primary life goals:

getting closer to God, living with a high level of integrity, having a single marriage for life, pursuing a clear purpose for their lives, and experiencing good health.

They tend to be generous people, as well. They are a close second to the Captives in the amount of money they donate to charities and churches each year, giving about four times the national household average. They are more likely than other tribes (except the Captives) to help nonprofit and community organizations, and they also give an above-average amount of their time as volunteers. They do not invest much in helping the poor, but they seem especially invested in assisting the elderly and the sick.

Mormons frequently talk about matters related to politics, morality, and parenting: these are areas of particular interest and importance to them. When it comes to parenting, they are especially likely to be interested in effectively passing on their own faith and spiritual heritage to their offspring, as well as ensuring that their kids receive a good education.

POLITICS AND GOVERNMENT

Like the Captives, Mormons cling to a conservative political ideology. A majority (55 percent) are registered Republicans; only one-sixth (17 percent) are registered Democrats. And a majority are also conservative (56 percent), while a mere 3 percent deem themselves to be liberal.

These leanings are consistent with their recent voting history. In 2000, Mormons supported George W. Bush over Al Gore by a four-to-one margin. In 2004, they backed George W. Bush again, that time giving him a five-to-one margin over John Kerry.

The issues that galvanize Mormons tend to be moral and economic. For instance, topping their slate of issues to be addressed are abortion, immigration, AIDS policies, poverty, and handling consumer debt. They are also noteworthy for their firm support of Christian language and symbols in the public square. By large margins, they embrace Christian language on currency and in the Pledge, they favor allowing the Ten Commandments to be posted in federal buildings, and they fervently support constitutional amendments to restrict marriage to a man and a woman.

As they look to the future, they are most concerned about finding leaders who will consider the spiritual condition and tenor of the nation, the state of the family, and the need to take better care of our children.

WHAT MORMONS BELIEVE AND PRACTICE

The religious involvement and interest of Mormons are indisputably high—higher than that found among any tribe other than the Captives. Nine out of every ten LDS adherents contend that their religious faith is very important in their lives today. Almost as many (85 percent) argue that their lives have been significantly transformed by their faith.

But if the views and values of Mormons have seemed clear and consistent up to this point, once we dig beneath the surface in the faith realm, such clarity vanishes. While Mormons overwhelmingly align themselves with Christianity, many of their beliefs and practices diverge from orthodox Christian teachings. Naturally, they bristle at being labeled a cult.

The argument for including them within the body of Christian believers is based largely on their adoption of many traditional Christian beliefs and practices. For instance, they are heavily involved in church events and programs. They are the most likely of all the tribes to engage in fasting for religious reasons, to attend Sunday school classes, and to volunteer at their churches. They are twice as likely to tithe as are the Captives—and several times more likely than any other tribe. They are second only to the Captives in activities such as attending church services, participating in a weekday small group, reading the Bible, praying, and sharing their faith with others.

There are other factors that weigh in favor of their inclusion in the Christian community. More than nine out of ten believe that the Bible is a holy or sacred book. (Three-quarters of them rely upon the King James Version—the oldest and most traditional translation.) Similarly, more than nine out of ten say they have made a "personal commitment to Jesus Christ that is still important in their life today." More than four out of five Mormons possess an orthodox view of God. Almost the entire body of Mormons we interviewed affirm the miracles in the Bible (e.g., Noah surviving the Flood, Moses parting the Red Sea, Samson performing great acts of strength, Christ being born of a virgin, Jesus feeding the five thousand, Peter walking on water with Jesus, Christ turning water into wine, and Jesus being physically resurrected). And there is similar near-unanimous belief in the existence of angels, the fact that God created the universe, and the notion that God still does miracles today. Nearly nine out of ten believe that the main purpose of life is to love God with all one's heart, mind, strength and soul.

Also, in contrast to Americans in general, a large majority of Mormons believe that Satan exists, that the Holy Spirit exists, that Jesus lived a sinless life, that heaven refers to spending eternity in the presence of God, and that hell refers to spending eternity separated from Him.

But those who challenge the Christian credentials of Mormons focus on a body of beliefs and exhortations drawn from literature and teaching that is not part of the orthodox Christian vault. For instance, while most Mormons concede that the Bible is a holy book, only three out of ten of them believe it is totally accurate in the principles it teaches. In fact, two-thirds of them say it is the Word of God, but it contains many errors. A slight majority go so far as to say that the Bible teaches the same principles as other holy books, such as the Koran and Book of Mormon, using different stories and characters. Such thinking is anathema to Protestant and Catholic scholars and leaders.

Seven out of ten Mormons believe that the Book of Mormon is a sacred book and place it at an equal or higher level of credibility as the Bible. The combination of drawing lessons from the Bible, the Book of Mormon, and the teachings of the church leads to a works-oriented theology: salvation is a result of various behaviors prescribed by their doctrine. Only 13 percent of Mormons contend that salvation is based solely on the grace of God delivered through the sacrifice of Jesus Christ on the Cross. Many LDS adherents see their own activities working in tandem with the atoning death of Christ as their means to salvation. Ultimately, eternity in the presence of God is seen as something that is earned as much as it is offered as a free gift from God.

Besides a doctrine of salvation that differs from that of biblical Christianity, other perspectives concern traditional Christians. Among them are the fact that Mormons are more likely to believe that the Bible's message is "God helps those who help themselves," that there are some sins that cannot be forgiven by God, and that all faiths worship the same God despite using different names for that deity. Further, only one out of ten Mormons believes in the existence of the Trinity, and most Mormons do not believe that God is actively guiding human history.

LIFE AS QUASI-CHRISTIANS

In a way, Mormons are the Rodney Dangerfield of the Christian world: they don't get no respect from the orthodox Christian community. The status of Latter-day Saints as outsiders at best, and cult members at worst, is largely driven by the angst of the Captives, who point out substantial differences between orthodox Christians and Mormons in critical dimensions such as the standing of the Bible, the role of Jesus Christ, the means to eternal salvation, the source of moral truth, the legitimacy of the revelations to Mormon leaders, and the like.

The aggressive and continual criticism of the Mormon faith by the Captives has affected the health of the LDS church. Some potential converts have been scared away by the barrage of negative publicity and incessant questions about Mormonism. Some

LDS members have been convinced that the LDS theology and practice are in error. But many Mormons have been driven into a closer, more cohesive community by the attacks from the outside, enabling them to jell as an oppressed, attacked minority group that interprets those attacks as evidence that they are legitimately serving God and are experiencing the promised persecution for their faith.

Whatever the external circumstances and confrontations may be, the data clearly show that Mormons are a spiritually inclined, devout group that centers its focus on family life and spiritual community. They are likely to continue growing in the coming decades because they have clarity about their beliefs and commitment to their leadership structure and internal procedures. They also have maintained an image of clean living (apart from the occasional polygamy flare-ups within splinter groups) and emphasize healthy family and community life. These are attractive elements, especially in a nation where theological distinctives are of limited interest to the average person.

CHAPTER
SIX
Pantheists:
People of Different Gods

IF THE MORMONS are the Rodney Dangerfields of the religious spectrum because they get no respect, then Pantheists are the Baskin-Robbins of the field: they have a flavor to suit everybody's taste.

Pantheism in America includes a wide range of faith groups: Hindu, Buddhist, Confucian, and a wealth of groups that fall under the generic New Age banner. A common thread is that all of these groups embrace spiritual perspectives that originated in Eastern cultures. While there is no single segment within this tribe that dominates—or that surpasses one-half of one percent in size—the entire collection of Eastern-oriented segments constitutes about 1.5 percent of the U.S. population.

One of the oddities of these groups is that they do not think of "God" as a personal, living entity. They are more likely to think of "god" as implying some system of power and authority rather than a personal force that has an impact on their lives.

A substantial majority of the nation's Pantheists are men. Members of this tribe are predominantly Asian (57 percent) and are more likely to live in the Pacific states (where the Asian population is largest). They are also an advertiser's dream: much younger than average and very upscale. Nearly six out of ten Pantheists have a college degree.

With a dozen or more different strains of Pantheism existing in America, identifying a specific set of spiritual practices and doctrines is not feasible. But they share a general way of perceiving and responding to the world that produces many common traits in terms of background, lifestyle, and attitudes.

HOW PANTHEISTS SEE THEMSELVES

While this tribe is defined on the basis of its spiritual perspectives and commitments, Pantheists are not an overly spiritual lot. Just half of them (54 percent) claim to be deeply spiritual. Only three out of ten from this tribe deem themselves to be full-time servants of God—a condition that is barely half as common as is found among the rest of Americans.

Pantheists are not moralists either. They are less concerned about the moral condition of the nation than are most tribes. This is related to the fact that they were next to the bottom in terms of supporting traditional family values; their values are anything but conventional. Overall, they do not fancy themselves to be upholders of the status quo in any way, shape, or form.

In fact, one of their most unique self-views is that they deem themselves to be social activists, risk takers, and people seeking to bring about change in the world. Even though they do not portray themselves as leaders, they often perform leadership tasks, such as bringing about change to facilitate progress.

What is intriguing about Pantheists is that they are more likely to describe self-imagery that they reject than to define components that they embrace. This is because they do not spend a lot of time reflecting on the meaning and purpose of life; they are more intent on living "in the moment" and doing whatever comes naturally than in spending a lot of time planning their future or developing an image.

A fair profile of Pantheists, then, might simply be that they are people trying to get the most out of life without forcing the issue. They strive to be content, experimental, open-minded, and eager to be surprised by life.

HOW PANTHEISTS THINK AND LIVE

Pantheists are not goal-driven people; they are reactive as much as proactive. Their lives may seem less predictable than most because they have few set outcomes to which they are devoted and love the freedom that comes with believing that life does not place boundaries on them. Any limitations are usually self-imposed.

If they are pressed to identify their priorities in life, family is the one most likely to emerge, even though a minority of Pantheists would name it as their dominant consideration. Living in comfort or experiencing success is the runner-up priority—and Pantheists are the tribe most likely to list comfort, adventure, and success as their highest ends in life. Their most treasured life objectives include developing their character, having good friendships, protecting their health, experiencing comfort, and earning a college degree. However, in comparison to other tribes, they are also much more likely to desire some of the accoutrements of the good life, such as having high-paying jobs (twice the national average), traveling the world for pleasure (twice the national average), owning large homes (double the national average), owning the latest household electronics (two-and-a-half times the national average), and having satisfying sexual relationships. The goals at the bottom of their list are those related to spirituality, fame, and traditional marriage and family.

Family is an interesting reality among Pantheists. Marriage rates are below average—partly because the members of this tribe are younger than the norm, but even more so because of their values. Rather than get married, members of this tribe are prone to cohabit. By the same token, Pantheists have the lowest desire of any tribe to have children and are also near the top of the scale in terms of engaging in sexual relations outside marriage. The values system of Pantheists is a pastiche of clichés: live and let live, take care of number one, if it feels good do it, live in such a way that you have no regrets.

Driven to experience comfort, Pantheists generally refuse to be encumbered by traditional expectations. As noted, their ideas about family clash with the common notions: they don't feel compelled to marry or to have children, and they are comfortable living with others and having sexual relations with many people. They do not get locked into causes or careers. They believe relationships are important, but not to the extent that such ties might hinder their eternal search for fun and fulfillment. In their lives, freedom and independence trump responsibility, reliability, and loyalty.

Not surprisingly, relatively few Pantheists (26 percent) believe there is such a thing as absolute moral truth. They are among the most ardent proponents of relativism. Their dominant source of truth is within: whatever they feel or sense is their primary guide for making moral choices.

In some ways, Pantheists are the ultimate pop culture aficionados. They are early adopters of technology; they feel a need to have all the electronic toys available. They stay on top of trends in the celebrity world, see more movies than any other tribe, and are constantly on the Internet. They are not big readers, but they greatly enjoy watching television, especially sitcoms, sports, and news-oriented programming. It never occurs to them to change the channel because of the moral content in the shows they watch; in their minds, it's all just entertainment, and every philosophy or message is just as valid as any other.

Among their tendencies is frequenting psychics. They are more likely than any other Americans to believe that such people have tapped into a real power and have a genuine skill for telling the future and dispensing viable advice. In fact, Pantheists are ten times as likely as the typical adult to visit a psychic in an average month.

Pantheists seem to be personable, outgoing people. They are less likely than most adults to engage in gossip and twice as likely to get drunk. They get immersed in conversation, but some topics such as morals, money, and parenting are generally off-limits.

Those subjects are simply too personal or, in some cases, uninteresting. They share an affinity with most Americans for discussing politics, entertainment news, and even matters of faith.

One of the paradoxes of members of this tribe is that despite their parting with traditional moral views, they are no more likely than the norm to gamble, view pornography, use profanity in public, or use tobacco products. They have no moral qualms about those elements; they simply have no greater appetite for them than do other people who might struggle with the morality of those behaviors.

Another paradox is that although they view poverty as one of the most significant issues facing the country today, they have no personal interest in getting involved with the poor or with programs designed to address poverty. Perhaps this has something to do with their own tendency to avoid debt; although they are free spenders, they do better than most at staying within their self-imposed spending limits.

POLITICS AND GOVERNMENT

An unusually small proportion of this tribe—64 percent, not quite two-thirds—are registered to vote. Among those who are registered, about half are aligned with the Democratic Party, a higher proportion than is found in the general population. Pantheists are more likely to be liberal than conservative (by a two-to-one margin), but two-thirds of them are middle-of-the-road in their ideological leanings. Because they tend to possess a laissez-faire approach to life, they are not usually intensely ideological.

In recent presidential elections, though, they have overwhelmingly sided with the more liberal Democratic candidates. In 2000, Pantheists supported Al Gore over George W. Bush by a two-to-one margin. Their distaste for the incumbent blossomed over the next four years, though, such that they backed John Kerry over George W. Bush by an eleven-to-one margin in 2004! Pantheists typically oppose any efforts to incorporate vestiges of faith—at least, the Christian faith—in public life. Whether it is retaining Christian precepts on currency, in the Pledge, or on the walls of government buildings, this tribe wants a faith-free environment. They also disdain the idea of teaching the Creation model in public schools. But they are not completely opposed to government involvement in their lives. For instance, by a five-to-one margin they oppose the *F* word being allowed in television programming and favor a law to that effect. They also desire greater government assistance in procuring rights for gays and lesbians, even though our data show that Pantheists are no more likely than people of other tribes to be homosexual or bisexual.

WHAT PANTHEISTS BELIEVE AND PRACTICE

The fact that Pantheists are among the least likely people in the nation to say they are deeply spiritual does not mean that they lack opinions about various aspects of faith and religion.

As would be expected of people who do not have any enduring links to the Judeo-Christian heritage or theological moorings, Pantheists generally dismiss much of the basis of the Christian and Jewish faiths. For instance, Pantheists do not believe that Jesus Christ was a holy or supernatural being. Nor do they believe that Satan exists or the Holy Spirit is real. Their idea of divinity is not based upon a single, supernatural entity with special powers, so they typically dispute the orthodox Christian perception of God. They do not accept the existence of angels or demons, and they dismiss the notions of heaven and hell.

The Bible fares no better. Although one out of every five Pantheists considers the Bible a holy book, the vast majority view it simply as a collection of stories written by men that contains numerous errors. They do not accept it as inspired by a supernatural deity, nor do they deem it to contain a body of life-changing principles.

Pantheists are a divided lot on the matter of sacred literature.

There is no particular work that a majority defend as holy or sacred. The book that comes closest to that standing is the Bhagavad Gita, one of the cherished works of the Hindu faith, which about three out of every ten Pantheists describe as holy. The Teachings of the Buddha has similar status among two out of every ten Pantheists, along with the Bible. Reflecting the diverse views of this tribe, however, we found that there were more than fifteen different pieces of "sacred literature" identified by Pantheists—the only tribe whose members listed more than a handful of such works.

While Pantheists are not necessarily well versed in the content of the holy books of various faith traditions, they overwhelmingly believe that all of the major examples of sacred literature—the Bible, Koran, Book of Mormon, and others—teach the same lessons and principles. This conforms to their notion that all faiths teach the same foundational principles and virtues, using different stories, characters, and ideas about an ultimate power or authority. American Pantheists hold to this universalist perspective by a four-to-one margin over those who acknowledge the theological distinctions of the major tribes. To the mind of the typical Pantheist, those distinctions are relatively insignificant; what matters is self-perfection, which they see as an objective of all genuine faith systems.

Given these views, it is not surprising to find that Pantheists dismiss a number of other Judeo-Christian ideas, as well. For example, only one-quarter of them agree that the primary purpose of life is to love God with all your heart, mind, strength, and soul. Just one out of five accepts the notion of humans having souls that live eternally. They contend that the Christian concept of original sin is false; instead, four out of five Pantheists believe that people make a choice to be good or bad and have the power to determine their response to any situation. Just one out of every eight Pantheists argues that true success is being obedient to God—and the 12 percent who believe this are not speaking about doing the will of the Christian God, but rather doing what is in concert with their own notion of a divine presence within themselves.

So Pantheists do not think of their faith system as something that has significantly transformed their lives; only three out of every ten Pantheists embrace such thinking. Rather, they think of their faith as something that gives them perspective on life and enables them to become better world citizens. Their faith challenges them to adopt positive principles about humanity and about the meaning of life, but those are not principles related to the involvement of a living, supernatural power. Their point of view is that the real power comes from within us, and their faith system exists to help unlock the power and wisdom that we naturally harbor.

Toward that end, Pantheists are less likely to consistently attend special religious events or instructional opportunities provided by their tribe. Instead, they participate in individualized spiritual pursuits such as prayer and meditation, and perhaps reading some of the sacred literature of their branch of Pantheism. They do not relate to practices such as tithing. Indeed, Pantheists give away very little money (an average of three hundred dollars per year, substantially less than the national average), and give less to religious institutions (about thirty-six dollars per year) than any tribe other than the Skeptics. They are more likely to see their money as a tool that they are personally responsible for managing in ways that balance personal good and common good, but without any specific pressures or obligations stemming from their religious teachings.

The faith journey of most Pantheists in America is a rather solitary experience. The sense of community is a general understanding of the existence of other like-minded people, rather than a physical community fortified by regular meetings, projects, programs, classes, and other institutional-driven activities. Pantheism is not strongly institutional; it is highly individual.

That rampant individualism is one reason why the experience of Pantheists is so varied. We know the following about them:

- They believe in multiple gods about which humans know little.
- The core perspectives of their belief systems change over the course of time.
- There is not a unified belief system that ties everything together.
- The numerous varieties of each branch of Pantheism (e.g., Buddhist sects such as Zen, Pure Land, Tibetan, Shingon, Mahayana; Hindu sects such as Shaivism, Smartha, Shaktism, Vaishnavism) embrace different interpretations of core concepts, which makes comprehension of the faith system even more difficult.
- An underlying principle is that life itself is an illusion, so there is little attempt to be intellectually rigorous.
- Each individual experiences a unique and unpredictable path to self-perfection.
- There are no creeds that provide a consistent passage of central truths, wisdom, or expectations.
- Time and life are cyclical, affected by each person's past (karma).
- Perfection is more likely when the individual is able to deny desire and overcome ignorance toward achieving greater detachment from the illusions of this world.

The ultimate objective that Pantheists share is that of freedom from the meaningless lures of this world and the achievement of peace with the universe. The means to that end vary within each branch of the tribe.

Our studies indicate that most Pantheists in America are moderately committed to pursuing the enlightenment their faith professes. Like all Americans, they struggle with materialism, lust, morality, integrity, love, suffering, and perseverance. Without a body of parameters to help them navigate the challenges of daily life or a community of fellow travelers to encourage them, many Pantheists struggle to make progress. But they appear to gain some self-assurance and peace from the fact that if they do not make as much progress on this leg of their journey as they had hoped, they will be recycled and given another opportunity to move closer to their ultimate outcome.

CONCLUSIONS

Because Pantheism is based on an entirely different set of philosophical standards than Christianity, Judaism, or Islam, most Americans are confused by Pantheism and dismiss it as a bizarre collection of nonsensical, disconnected, quasispiritual thoughts. However, with the growth of the Asian population in the United States, and the move toward globalization, it is likely that Pantheism will continue to gain ground in this country.

While the faith wars swirl around them, Pantheists often stay removed from the fray, disinterested in the nitpicking, hostility-fueling schisms over what to believe and how to promote their own preferences. They typically are focused on how to make personal progress toward their own perfection.

Pantheists face several uphill struggles for broader acceptance in America. First, because their numbers are relatively minuscule, they lack visibility. Second, because their faith system operates from a completely different foundation, they are misunderstood and offhandedly dismissed as not having a serious faith. Third, lacking a recognized body of leaders or advocates within the culture, they have little voice. Fourth, the very disinterest in competition to elevate the profile and acceptance of their faith makes it hard for Pantheist perspectives to gain a hearing and a foothold in the United States. And finally, because they are not a cohesive community, they miss out on the opportunity to participate in many of the faith adventures that advance the role of spirituality in America.

Nevertheless, Pantheists provide an interesting counterbalance to the Judeo-Christian perspectives and practices embraced by 87 percent of the nation.

CHAPTER
SEVEN
Muslims in America

MUSLIMS have struggled with their image in America for the better part of the past half century. The Muslim faith was simply a foreign religion to most Americans until the late 1950s. At that time a young, charismatic Muslim preacher in New York named Malcolm X introduced large numbers of Americans to the Muslim faith. Among the doctrines he taught were pride in African heritage and hatred toward whites, Jews, and Christians.

In the late 1960s, the Black Muslims emerged as a radical activist group that challenged the status quo—and especially the oppression of African Americans—in the United States. Associated with violence and anarchy, their image was predominantly negative in the white-majority nation. In the midsixties, the Black Panthers grabbed national headlines as leaders like Bobby Seale and Huey Newton campaigned for greater rights for African Americans, following the Black Muslim teachings of Malcolm X. The 1968 Olympics were the scene of another memorable event, when U.S. medal winners Tommie Smith and John Carlos raised their gloved hands in protest during the medal ceremony. While Smith denies he was connected with the Black Muslims, many assumed his gesture conveyed support for the movement, bringing the Muslim community to the forefront once again.

The sports scene was one of the most visible places where role models for young Americans extolled the virtues of the Muslim faith. During the 1960s and 1970s a stream of high-profile athletes began changing their names to Muslim ones. World heavyweight boxing champion Cassius Clay became Muhammad Ali. Basketball great Lew Alcindor became Kareem Abdul-Jabbar. Numerous players in professional baseball, basketball, football, and boxing followed suit.

In 1995, Louis Farrakhan and his Nation of Islam organization emerged with his news-grabbing Million Man March through the nation's capital, again raising fears among the white population as to what African American men were protesting and how they planned to change the country to their liking. It was the largest organized march in Washington, D.C., history. Farrakhan was another disciple of the radical activist Malcolm X.

Then, in the aftermath of September 11, 2001, when America experienced the first attack on its home soil by an enemy since the Revolutionary War, the culprits were simply characterized as Muslims. Once again, Muslims were viewed as hostile to American interests—this time through acts of terrorism that led to the United States declaring war against Afghanistan and Iraq, with a special plan for retaliation against the al Qaeda sect. For many Americans, the Muslim faith became known as the religion of violence and hatred.

This tribe is now a collection of vastly differing Muslim segments, each with a different history and varying theological perspectives. As a result, the Muslim community in America is the most ethnically balanced of all: one-quarter black, one-fifth Asian, two-fifths white, and one-sixth mixed and other backgrounds. It is also the only tribe that can claim two-thirds of its adherents as foreign-born. Muslims are concentrated in the northeastern states: half live in that region. People associated with the Muslim faith also tend to be younger than the norm: a majority of Muslim adults in the United States are under the age of forty.

HOW MUSLIMS SEE THEMSELVES

The faith of Muslims is inseparable from their self-image. More than three out of five (62 percent) say they are "deeply spiritual." In fact, two-thirds are more likely to see themselves as Muslims than as Americans: their identity is spiritual more than nationalistic.

While they harbor average stress levels, Muslims do not have the same levels of happiness and satisfaction as do people from most other tribes. This may have to do with their sense of being rejected and even persecuted by American society. A majority (54 percent) believe that government policies single out Muslims. Even more of them contend that news coverage is unfair toward Muslims and the Islamic faith. One-third say they have experienced one or more forms of intolerance in the past year. With this type of burden, it is no wonder Muslims struggle to find peace and joy in life.[20]

An unusually high percentage of the tribe (40 percent) describe themselves as social activists. This is probably a reflection of their felt need to speak out against the discrimination they experience. They have a desire to change Americans' perceptions of Muslims, fearing that they are commonly viewed as terrorists and that Americans possess a skewed understanding of the Islamic faith. They would like to correct those misunderstandings.

Overall, Muslims see themselves as hardworking, peace-loving, moral people who place a premium on family life. They believe that education is one of the routes to success in life; many Muslims relocated to the United States specifically to benefit from the country's educational system.

WHAT MUSLIMS THINK

Compared to members of other tribes, American Muslims are somewhat restless. They have a lower sense of peace with life. More of them than would be found in other tribes are actively seeking to figure out their meaning and purpose in life. They are intent upon living meaningful lives and do not want to miss out on significant opportunities or their assigned purposes from Allah.

The most important elements in the life of Muslims are their faith and families. Owing to their relatively young average age, a higher proportion of Muslims have children in their household than is found in any other tribe: about six out of ten have youngsters under the age of eighteen in their homes. Training their children in Muslim doctrine and traditions is a vital part of their commitment.

Muslims generally believe in the American dream. Seven out of ten say that people who work hard can usually get ahead in the United States. Two-thirds of Muslims are comfortable pursuing that dream, seeing no conflict between being a Muslim and living in American society.

Muslims generally embrace conservative positions on lifestyle issues. For instance, they are generally against abortion and homosexuality, and they support public policies designed to limit such activities. They tend to see pornography as a blight on society and would favor bans on accessibility to such content. They also have serious reservations about the material provided by the media, contending that it corrupts minds, especially those of young people.

As might be expected, most Muslims appreciate the freedom enjoyed in American society but also feel more comfortable with well-defined gender and family roles. Even though most Muslims do not wear religious items or traditional Muslim clothing, they would prefer that Americans dress more modestly.

Perhaps unexpectedly, Muslims overwhelmingly favor relative moral truth to a commitment to the existence and implementation of absolute moral truth. This tribe embraces relativism by a two-to-one margin. Even though Muslims are often thought to hold fast to a rigid moral code, American Muslims generally believe that individuals must be allowed to interpret circumstances and Islamic law on their own.

HOW MUSLIMS LIVE

The lifestyle of Muslims is modest. They are about 40 percent less likely than other Americans to own their homes, so their space is often limited, and they tend to be somewhat more mobile than people of other tribes. They are not particularly interested in technology, lagging behind all other tribes in possession of computer, video, and audio electronics, and they are also less likely to have high-speed Internet connections at home.

Life is complicated for many Muslims. While they generally attempt to adopt as many American customs as possible, they are selective about those they embrace. They want to be accepted as part of American society, yet about half of all Muslims admit that all or most of their friends are fellow Muslims.[21] They have televisions, but they view less programming than average, and they are more likely than most adults to turn off content they find morally unacceptable. They pursue education, but they are over 50 percent more likely than other Americans to homeschool their children while they are young. For Muslims in America, the transition to the mainstream is in process but far from finished.

One of the joys of living in the United States is the freedom to speak their minds. Muslims do this with relish. They are more likely than most citizens to discuss moral matters, faith issues, and family concerns.

Often, however, the lifestyle of Muslims speaks even louder than their words. Compared to other tribes they are considerably less likely to view pornography, commit adultery, get drunk, gamble, buy lottery tickets, or seek advice from psychics. They are less likely than average to get divorced too. Despite their preference for moral relativism, they typically opt for rather conservative individual behavioral choices.

Muslims want to live the good life, but such an existence is defined largely by their religious beliefs. Consequently, their dominant life goals reflect a rather traditional mind-set. For instance, their primary goals include living with integrity, getting closer to Allah, having satisfying sexual relationships with their spouses (and only their spouses), experiencing good health, and having good close friends. They have little interest in fame, technology, and success. They are even less interested than most in being active in their religious centers (i.e., mosques).

Life is not all structure and seriousness for Muslims though. The number of movies they see in theaters each year is more than double the national average.

POLITICS AND GOVERNMENT

Many Muslims are not yet American citizens, which helps explain why so few are registered to vote (just 65 percent, well below the national average of 81 percent). Despite their conservative lifestyles, a majority of Muslims are registered Democrats; only one out of every ten is a Republican. Ideologically, liberals outnumber conservatives 23 percent to 15 percent (leaving a large majority in the middle-of-the-road segment).

The Democratic Party preference has been clearly demonstrated among the Muslims who voted in recent presidential elections. In 2000, Muslims sided with Al Gore over George W. Bush by a two-to-one margin. That gap grew substantially by 2004, when Muslims supported John Kerry over George W. Bush by a five-to-one differential.

What makes Muslims "liberal"? Perhaps their consistent viewpoint that government should be more active in American life. For instance, 70 percent prefer bigger government that will provide more public services. Three out of four say government should do more to assist the poor. Six out of ten want government to play a bigger role in protecting traditional moral values in the United States.[22]

Muslims are almost evenly divided as to whether they want mosques to stay out of politics or be involved in the process. Much like other Americans, they can see value in integrating religious values into the public policy arena, but they are also cognizant of the dangers such a mixing of politics and religion could create.

WHAT MUSLIMS BELIEVE AND PRACTICE

Muslims are religious people: more than three-fourths of them (78 percent) describe their religious faith as very important in their lives today. But their religious activity is most often practiced in private rather than in the midst of religious events. The most widespread Islamic practice in America is daily prayer, which more than three out of five engage in. Muslims are more likely than any other tribe to fast for religious reasons. They are also the most generous financial givers of all tribes, donating roughly five times the national average to nonprofits and religious entities.

A recent national survey by the Pew Research Center provides significant insight into the religious views of Muslims in the United States. Among their findings were the following:

- 96 percent believe in Allah alone;
- 94 percent believe in the Prophet Muhammad;
- 91 percent believe there will be a day of judgment;
- 87 percent believe in angels;
- 77 percent say fasting during Ramadan is very important;
- 76 percent contend that giving to charity is very important;
- 63 percent state that making a pilgrimage to Mecca is very important.[23]

To more completely understand Muslims, realize that they are not evangelistically inclined. They fervently cherish the opportunity to practice their faith without limitations, but our studies find that only about one-third of Muslims say they feel it is very important to share their beliefs with non-Muslims.

The eternal hope of Muslims lies partly on the shoulders of

Allah and partly on their own. Three out of every four Muslims believe it is important to be good people and do good things for others so they can earn their way to eternal salvation. Few Muslims (one-third) believe that Satan exists, so there are no spiritual forces standing in their way of goodness; it is purely a personal decision as to how to act.

Knowing exactly how to "do and be good" is made more challenging by the widespread belief among Muslims that the Koran, their holy book, can be interpreted in various ways. While four-fifths of Muslims say the Koran is definitely the word of God, only half say it must be interpreted literally.

In the end, Muslims are proud of their faith and say that it guides their lives. In total, seven out of ten Muslims believe their faith has significantly transformed their lives. Most of them remain uncertain but hopeful about their ultimate destinies.

CHANGES COMING IN THE FUTURE

If history is any indication of what is ahead for the Islamic community in America—and the past continues to be the best predictor of the future—then we might expect to see Muslims struggling with a variety of moral and spiritual challenges posed by pop culture. Ours is a land of endless distractions, diversions, and seductions that tend to draw people away from their moral centers. Purity of belief or behavior is a challenge whose difficulty is constantly underestimated.

What makes the outcome for American Muslims so hard to predict is the fact that their tribe is, in essence, a first-generation community. With immigration primarily responsible for their growth in numbers, it will take another thirty to fifty years to determine whether the Muslim faith in the Unites States will retain its traditions and core beliefs. Our society is prone to try to distort everything with which it has contact, so it will push, probe, tease, and tempt Islam to adapt to American ways. These next few decades will certainly be a struggle for Muslims.

Strangely, one factor this tribe has working in its favor is the persecution that Muslims endure in our nation. Those pressures and prejudices will embolden Muslims to band together and resist many of the culture's temptations. How their character and strength fare over the long haul is yet to be ascertained, but the crucible of hostility they believe they face will surely help them push back with greater determination and solidarity.

CHAPTER
EIGHT
Spiritual Skeptics

AROUND the world, the United States is widely considered to be one of the most religious nations, filled primarily with Christians. What gets relatively little attention is the fact that one out of every ten citizens (11 percent) are either atheist (9 percent) or agnostic (2 percent). That is an important distinction, by the way. Atheists are those who contend with certainty that God does not exist; they do not believe in Him or that anything that exists can be attributed to Him. Agnostics are people who hold that God may exist, but that it is impossible for human beings to know with certainty. Atheists rely upon arguments that they believe poke holes in theist positions supporting the existence of God or His creation of the universe. Agnostics believe that neither position can be proven, so they keep their spiritual options open.[24]

The combination of atheists and agnostics gains a lot of attention in religious research circles. What receives less attention is that the group has nearly doubled in size during the past quarter century, currently representing about twenty-five million adults. Given the current spiritual patterns evident in the research, we anticipate continued, significant growth of this tribe.

Skeptics—the name I have assigned to the tribe that blends atheists and agnostics—are most heavily concentrated along the East and West Coasts, although they are present throughout the nation. They are the least likely people among all the tribes to get married (just 44 percent are presently married) and are among the most likely to be homosexual (almost double the national average). This tribe is comprised of an unusually high percentage of men (57 percent) and Asians. (Skeptics are twice as likely as other Americans to be Asian.) African Americans are notably less likely to be part of this tribe (just 8 percent are African American).

Human nature seeks a natural enemy, and for many Americans of faith, the Skeptics constitute such a foe. Years ago, it was common for people to refer to Skeptics as un-American because of their godless philosophy. The culture has changed dramatically, however, with organizations such as the American Civil Liberties Union and Americans United for Separation of Church and State, which consistently seek to remove God as well as other religious (especially Christian) symbols, language, and ideals from public life.

The assumption of people aligned with other tribes is often that Skeptics are unscrupulous, unrefined, amoral individuals. Our research over the course of the past quarter century indicates that such stereotypes are inaccurate. There are significant differences between the faithful and the faithless, but the research shows that those distinctions may be different than many people imagine.

HOW SKEPTICS SEE THEMSELVES

In many ways, Skeptics see themselves as typical Americans, and there is ample evidence to support that perspective. They have average stress levels and are just as likely as others to describe themselves as busy, reliable, loyal, self-sufficient, skeptical, and misunderstood. They have the same difficulties as everyone else when it comes to making and keeping friends. They are no more—or less—likely than others to want control over their lives, to enjoy making tough decisions, to like having new experiences, and to believe that they cope well with challenges.

They do pride themselves, however, in being different from the pack in some respects. For instance, they are more likely than other adults to place their careers above all other activities in their lives. They also like the challenges brought about by change and don't mind taking risks to have unique adventures or breakthroughs. In that respect, they are more likely than most to contend that they adapt easily to changes and challenges.

Skeptics are comfortable creating or dealing with conflict. This mind-set goes hand in hand with their self-image as people who are insensitive to social pressure. For the most part, these people pursue their own vision of life and don't put much stock in what others think; their commitment is to be true to self rather than to compromise in order to be part of a larger community or movement.

However, Skeptics are not a class of type A personalities. They are less likely than average to see themselves as leaders, as being fully committed to getting ahead in the world, or as individuals devoted to fulfilling a specific life calling. To the contrary, they are simply trying to live with integrity based on what they believe—even if their belief systems lack a deity or higher power.

As you might expect, the dimension in which they most radically differ from the rest of the tribes is the spiritual realm. While these folks do not believe in God, a notable number of them possess some spiritual inclinations. One-quarter of the Skeptics adopt the label "deeply spiritual" (which is distinct from being religious). There is an intriguing connection between the lack of spiritual emphasis of Skeptics and the fact that they report feeling lower levels of joy and peace with life. They also are less likely to believe they are making a difference in the world. They are among the most likely to say they lack spiritual maturity. The difference between them and members of other tribes is that it doesn't bother the Skeptics.

An outgrowth of their diminished emphasis upon spirituality is that fewer Skeptics are actively searching for a better understanding of the meaning and purpose in their lives. Only a little more than one-third are seeking such clarity. A majority of them (about six out of ten) describe the meaning of life as "work hard, do well, enjoy life however you can."

By and large, Skeptics do not spend much time pondering the grand themes of existence; they are content to try to live in the moment and accept life for what it is without much philosophizing about what it was meant to be or where it is all going. The data show that Skeptics are, in fact, less likely than others to have a clear sense of their life purpose, but that admission of ignorance is just as likely to reflect their contention that life has no purpose as it is to suggest they are baffled as to what it might be.

It is worth noting that a large number of the Captives have become accustomed to referring to people such as the Skeptics as "lost." Our research found that a large majority of the Skeptics resent being characterized in that manner since it is not only a pejorative term but also insinuates that they are definitely wrong and somehow defective. The irony is that evangelistic Christians use that phrase in their efforts to win over nonbelievers, when the phrase itself repulses nonbelievers and precludes them from even hearing the overtures of Christians.

HOW SKEPTICS THINK AND LIVE

One of the hallmarks of Skeptics is their desire simply to get on with life. They spend little time agonizing over public issues and problems. Overall, they want to make the most of their time on earth and believe there is little to be gained from investing themselves in improving the world. (In fact, only one out of every three Skeptics is interested in helping to make the world a better place.) In their worldview, history is random and impersonal, giving them little impetus to act as if what they do has eternal consequences or any large-scale meaning.

They have very limited confidence in the morals and character of institutional leaders. They have concerns about the moral condition of the United States but not much hope that it will change. In fact, despite their interest in addressing matters related to social justice, poverty, and environmental conditions, most of them say they would not change much of anything about their lives—past, present, or future. That includes letting the chips fall as they may in relation to family, faith, media, morality— pretty much everything.

Most Skeptics believe there are no absolute moral truths: less than one out of every five accept the existence of moral absolutes. Instead, they believe that truth can be ascertained only through experience, reason, and logic, and that it varies from situation to situation. They buy this view so strongly that eight out of ten of them teach their own kids relativism; just 4 percent even raise the possibility that absolutes may exist. When it comes time to make critical moral choices, they rely on their feelings and experiences to guide them.

Besides supporting the idea that there are no moral absolutes, Skeptics have some well-defined views of other faiths. The dominant American faith—Christianity—is something they perceive to be unappealing. Specifically, two-thirds or more of the Skeptic population describe Christianity as judgmental, old-fashioned, out of touch with reality, and insensitive to other people. The fact that more than three-quarters of Skeptics see Christians as hypocritical further dampens their willingness to take what the group says seriously.

So in the process of doing what they feel is right, they often operate alone. Skeptics, more than most tribes, feel disconnected from other people. They do not have the sense of community that shared religious beliefs and practices provide for many Americans. While they acknowledge that certain people— namely, teachers, family members, and friends—have had the greatest impact on their lives, they also feel somewhat distant from all of those people. They are the only tribe that places a greater premium on their work associations than on their ties to

THE SEVEN FAITH TRIBES / GEORGE BARNA

family and friends, even though they mention taking care of and enjoying their family as their highest priority in life.

Given these attitudes and values, life looks and feels different for Skeptics than for people in other tribes. Among the things they most look forward to are a good night of sleep and access to their favorite music. They are less likely than other tribes to spend time with friends. And when they do share such moments, they are no more likely than anyone else to become immersed in meaningful discussions of matters such as politics or parenting or faith. They live in the moment and move on, without a great deal of emotion—or fulfillment.

Befitting their "typical American" status, Skeptics share some lifestyle patterns with most Americans. For example, their levels of involvement with gambling, psychics, and irresponsible spending are nearly identical to that of other U.S. adults. They enjoy technology and entertainment, but their consumption levels are merely equivalent to those of other tribes.

Even their life goals are similar to those of many Americans. The top-rated goals of Skeptics include enjoying good health, living with integrity, having a few close friends, experiencing a satisfying sex life with their spouses, and living in comfort. They show a decided lack of interest in achieving fame, owning the latest and greatest technology, and being involved in a church or other spiritual activity. With the exception of that latter component, this profile could describe most of the tribes in America.

The most overt differences between Skeptics and people from other tribes are in the areas of speech, sexuality, and substance use. They admit to having a tendency to lie, gossip, and use profanity in public. They are twice as likely as other adults to engage in adultery, are more likely to cohabit, and are the major consumers of pornography. They are also much more likely than people from other tribes to drink excessively. Some analysts have said these behaviors are nonsensical for a group that is striving to simply fit in with the crowd and optimize the moment. But in fact, these behaviors make complete sense given their beliefs that there are no absolute moral standards, that there is no deity to answer to, and that there is no judgment or life after death dependent upon their performance in life.

These tendencies bother people from other tribes more than they do the Skeptics because their moral compass is set to a different true north. Lacking any absolutes to guide them, Skeptics are inclined to do what feels appropriate in a given situation, even if it conflicts with cultural mores. So they don't worry about movie ratings or popularity; they select films to watch because they find them appealing. They donate less money to causes and offer less help to disadvantaged people than any other tribe, but only because their sense is that everyone makes his or her own choices and needs to deal with the consequences created by those choices. They rarely, if ever, censor the media they or their children watch, assigning all media and entertainment content equal validity. In fact, Skeptics are the only tribe in which parents generally allow their children to set their own standards and limits regarding media consumption.

Two-thirds of the Skeptics say they live according to a set of core values they possess. There is no reason to doubt that. What confounds many people is the nature of those values.

Skeptics are also comfortable with ambiguity and messiness in life. Most of them have come to grips with their position that the existence of God is a question they will never definitely answer. Since a resolution to the central question of existence escapes them, they are more willing to concede that there will be other, less profound matters that may be beyond their grasp as well. Gray is an acceptable color to Skeptics.

POLITICS AND GOVERNMENT

Although Skeptics are less likely than average to be registered to vote (73 percent are registered, compared to 81 percent nationwide) and their turnout during elections is somewhat lower than the norm, their leanings are easy to follow. Three-quarters of them are registered as Democrats or independents, and they are nearly three times as likely to call themselves liberal as conservative.

Those tendencies produced substantial numbers of votes for two recent Democratic presidential nominees. In 2000, Skeptics were more likely to cast their ballots for Al Gore than for George W. Bush by a two-to-one margin. In 2004, the gap widened considerably, as they backed John Kerry over George W. Bush by a five-to-two ratio.

As would be expected, then, our studies have found that Skeptics are fervent supporters of gay rights and energetic opponents of the Federal Marriage Amendment (by a six-to-one differential). As people who either doubt or reject the existence of God, it is not surprising that they do not want creationism taught in the schools (by a four-to-one margin). They strongly favor abortion rights and firmly oppose parental notification if a minor is getting an abortion (67 percent oppose such a law).

Even their perspective on the identification of significant issues facing the nation is different from that of other tribes. For instance, they generally dismiss the idea that abortion, gay rights, immigration reform, and media morality are major issues. Perhaps surprisingly, they also emerged as the only tribe to consider terrorism to be a second-tier issue.

But just to make things interesting, Skeptics did not emerge as a tribe that was all-out against having "In God We Trust" on currency or "one nation under God" in the Pledge of Allegiance. And they seem rather ambivalent about allowing people to express their faith views in the workplace, with equal proportions of the tribe on each side of that discussion.

WHAT SKEPTICS BELIEVE

Although relatively few Skeptics argue that their faith is very important in their lives, our research has found some unexpected insights into their spiritual lives. Nearly half of the adults in this tribe describe themselves as faith seekers who are unattached to an organized body of faith or theological perspective. In fact, one out of every five Skeptics also claims to think about faith matters on a *daily* basis.

Also intriguing is the fact that so many Skeptics absorb religious media on a somewhat regular basis. One-quarter of them listen to religious radio programming during a typical month, one-sixth watch Christian television programming each month, and one-fifth have read a Christian book, other than the Bible, during the past year. In total, one-third (35 percent) are voluntarily exposed to religious media content during a typical month.

Perhaps the most stunning discovery of all, though, is that our studies have consistently shown that nearly one-third of Skeptics believe in an orthodox view of God. This pattern has even been acknowledged by the Skeptics Society based on some research they conducted among Skeptics regarding people's perceptions of God. Their study revealed that many confirmed agnostics believe that God does exist. The primary reasons for such belief are the existence of apparent patterns in nature and the universe that could not be explained apart from the involvement of a superior being, the comfort that belief provides to the believer, and the feeling that they have somehow experienced the presence of God in their midst.[25] As it turns out, these are exactly the same reasons—intelligent design, emotional and psychological relief, and personal experience—that lead most believers of other tribes to embrace their deity. Very few Americans believe in God because they feel there is solid proof for His existence; that, of course, is why it is called faith rather than certainty.

These revelations do not necessarily mean Skeptics are seeking to align with a more conventional faith tribe. Placed in context, these findings merely suggest that Skeptics engage in a substantial degree of reflection regarding the role and substance of faith in their lives. They are not so much trying to fill a perceived hole in their understanding of life as attempting to grasp the apparent appeal of faith to the masses.

There does not seem to be any urgency among Skeptics about diving into a more traditional faith experience. By an overwhelming five-to-two margin they believe it is possible to lead a satisfying life without investing in faith. And the substance of their beliefs confirms that most Skeptics do not seem poised to cross the boundary lines to join another tribe.

As you might predict, Skeptics dismiss concepts such as Satan, the Holy Spirit, the Trinity, angels, and demons. They believe that a person known as Jesus Christ lived on earth, but they do not believe that He was both human and divine, that He lived a sinless life, or that He had a physical resurrection.

Skeptics dismiss the Bible as literature written by men. They do not believe it is the Word of God, nor do they buy the notion that it provides essential principles for living a successful life. They are familiar with many of the miracles described in its pages—largely because most American Skeptics have had a season of life during which they were regular attenders of a Christian church—but they consider those stories to be inaccurate fables. When it comes to holy books, they are familiar with several—the Bible, Koran, Teachings of the Buddha, Torah, Bhagavad Gita—but do not deem any of them to be sacred.

The Skeptics' broad view of the faith world is that people aligned with the other six tribes are searching for something that adds value and direction to their lives—but that it is a futile quest. Skeptics contend that all of the major world religions teach the same principles, using different language and stories, to convey the same principles and ideals. From the Skeptics' point of view, however, most of those lessons are simply about living a good and pleasing life. Such lessons are not so much about the necessity of faith in supernatural powers, untapped personal power, or belief in great spiritual figures. They just present the essence of what it means to be a self-realized human being. Skeptics believe that because we all have the option of being good or bad and of determining the lifestyle we feel is appropriate and worth pursuing, faith may help us achieve those outcomes, but they see it as little more than a tool that assists us in achieving our desired ends.

Given that view, it is not surprising to find that a large majority of Skeptics say that all people experience the same outcome after death: absolute nothingness. It is surprising that one-third of them believe that people have an eternal soul, but apparently it does not have much of a role in this life or beyond.

Five of the tribes—Captives, Casuals, Jews, Mormons, and Muslims—describe sin as an offense against God. Skeptics see it as a way of describing inappropriate social behavior. Their definition of sin is decidedly narrower than that of any other tribe, but the concept of doing things that are inexcusable resonates with them. In this light, then, we can understand why Skeptics believe that sin remains a relevant concept for today's world—by a three-to-one ratio! Call it sin, crime, or evil, it's all the same to them.

CONFOUNDING THE PEOPLE OF FAITH

It has been said by some that it takes more faith to believe there is no higher power that created and controls the world than to accept the existence of such a deity. Whether that is true or not, we know from the research that most Americans feel sorry for the Skeptics, believing that they are missing out on the perspective that pulls everything together into a sensible point of view. To varying degrees, people in the other tribes don't understand how it is possible to be a Skeptic.

Because Skeptics have no statement of faith or other creed to which they subscribe, knowing how to think about and respond to them often confounds people from other tribes, especially those who are evangelistically or apologetically inclined. Further muddying the waters is the fact that some Skeptics are open to discussions about spirituality while others, especially the highly educated Skeptics who work as professors or in other philosophically oriented positions, are more interested in the process of debating faith matters than genuinely pondering various faith positions.

Any honest examination of the faith tribes of America, though, must include the Skeptics. In addition to the validity of their faith position, they play a valuable role in the aggregate faith community: asking tough questions and keeping the other tribes on their toes. Skeptics, for the most part, have no vested interest in what others believe; they tend to hold their own beliefs closely and not worry about converting others to their own position. (Yes, there are exceptions, some of whom have recently written best sellers defending their lack of belief in God.) In a very real way, Skeptics provide balance on the spiritual continuum, holding down one extreme while the Captives, Muslims, and Mormons hold down the other end regarding the existence of God.

CHAPTER
NINE
Calibrating Our Values and Worldview

IT IS always difficult for any group to take an objective look at itself and identify its shortcomings. Often it is even tougher to acknowledge the flaws that surface and do something about them. The alternative is to let things continue unaltered and bear the consequences of such intentional neglect.

Rather than asking the various faith tribes to accept the unacceptable, I am advocating that they admit that they possess significantly different worldviews, but that within the framework of those worldviews lies a base of values that we can all agree upon. The power of those shared values constitutes the glue that can hold this country together. And it is those same values that represent the bedrock on which good character is developed.

If we can harness the power of the media to focus on those shared values, rather than constantly striving to generate controversy around our differences, then we can begin to bridge the gap that has divided us and heal the wounds that have set us against each other. Young people have an expression: TMI ("too much information"). We would do well to apply that notion to our journalistic and media environments.

We are a country blessed with thousands of gifted leaders. Imagine what would happen if Americans no longer accepted glib but empty statements about the future and instead demanded that our leaders provide a compelling vision founded on our shared values. Imagine your own life in an environment in which everyone you encounter is devoted to fulfilling the same vision, and your own skills and abilities are maximized in its pursuit.

Would the United States be different if your life—and that of every other citizen—was focused upon a clear and dignified purpose that propelled you beyond mere survival or comfort? How would you feel about yourself, your country, and your life if you were motivated to reach your full potential?

Ask any athletic coach how to approach a team that is mired in a slump. Game after game produces losses, despite the presence of talented and committed athletes on the team. Is the best strategy just to wait it out? To give up? To develop a plan that alters the current approach? If you poll great coaches, they invariably say you have to change what you're doing to get better results. (Remember the definition of insanity: doing the same things over and over and expecting different results!)

We are in a national slump. We have the talent and the resources. We have ample information and analysis about our situation and the possibilities. We need a new game plan. Let's consider one.

THE POWER OF YOUR WORLDVIEW

America is comprised of more than 300 million people, each of whom has a different story and a unique dream. But one of the things we all have is a worldview. That's a fancy word for describing the mental filter we each use to make sense of the world and to respond in ways that are consistent with what we believe to be true and appropriate. Our worldview begins to develop as soon as we leave the womb and never stops developing, although its foundational elements are generally in place by the time we reach age thirteen.

Life is about making choices. Our choices are based upon the information we receive, the experiences we have, and our ability to interpret all of that input through some type of matrix that organizes the data and allows us to draw conclusions. As our world becomes increasingly complex, so does the process of decision making, which elevates the importance of our worldviews. We cannot effectively understand the choices that other people make unless we can identify the heart of their worldviews.

In fact, we are constantly making decisions through our worldviews and reacting to the decisions others have made in response to their worldviews. Let's take a couple of examples from daily experience.

At your local convenience store, lottery tickets are available for sale at the checkout counter.

- Muslims usually perceive playing the lottery to be a form of gambling, which their faith strictly prohibits. Most American Muslims avoid the lottery, recognizing that it is simply a distraction from Allah and a foolish waste of money. In their tribe, any form of gambling is a sin.
- Captive Christians believe they have the freedom to buy such chances but typically refuse to do so because they consider gambling to be inappropriate management of the money God has entrusted to them for higher purposes. It is also viewed as an attempt to get something for nothing, which is contrary to the biblical command to earn your way.
- Casual Christians would consider the opportunity without worrying much about its theological implications. They believe God doesn't much care how they spend their discretionary funds, and, besides, they might get lucky. (Some might go so far as to believe that God might use the lottery to bless them with a financial windfall.) Their major worry would be the potential for becoming addicted or for losing so much money that other basic needs might not be met; but if they believe they can control their gambling urges, they would not have a compelling spiritual reason *not* to play the lottery.

- Traditional Jewish teaching simply encourages adherents not to gamble as a profession and not to overdo participation in betting. Most American Jews do not think something as innocuous as buying a lottery ticket is gambling or spiritual. Their tendency is to regard it either as a potential investment or as entertainment.
- Mormons believe that hard work is the route to godliness and that gambling is a form of evil, so although they might occasionally buy a ticket, they generally dismiss such behavior as counterproductive and sinful.
- Pantheists, depending on which strain they come from, would probably be tempted and then resist, remembering that this is among the evil lures of the worldly system that seeks to entrap them in bad karma. Every once in a while, though, they might feel the urge and succumb. While the sacred texts are ambiguous about gambling, the crucial factor is self-control and discipline.
- Skeptics usually base their decision on their current financial situation and whether or not they feel lucky. Alternatively, some regularly buy tickets because they believe the odds are good that they will eventually win something (although probably not the jackpot).

Here's another example. Let's say you decide to attend the annual community celebration. The central portion of Main Street is blocked off and people from throughout the community come together to honor some townsfolk and to get to know each other. Tables and tables of foods of all kinds are provided for people's culinary enjoyment. But as you watch the parade of people, you notice some patterns. For instance, in deference to Jewish tradition and teaching, most Jews pass up the pork and shellfish. Muslims fear that Allah will refuse to hear their prayers if they eat pork. Mormons and Muslims contend that God is dishonored by the consumption of drinks that limit your self-control, such as caffeinated drinks (including coffee or cola) and alcohol. Pantheists tend to avoid beef because eating it produces bad karma. Captive Christians shy away from alcohol because it can cause them to lose mastery over their minds and bodies. Skeptics abstain from foods that their doctors have warned them to avoid for medical reasons.

And what about a controversial social issue such as homosexuality? Captive Christians, Muslims, and Mormons have nearly identical perceptions: homosexuality is an obscene sexual perversion and a sin against God. They believe God will punish homosexuals; Mormons reserve the right to excommunicate them. The Jewish community agonizes over the issue, some within the tribe believing it is legitimate if based on genuine love, others citing Torah law calling it an abomination before God. Pantheists are also somewhat divided within the tribe; although such behavior is permitted, it's generally discouraged. The bottom line is they acknowledge it as an individual choice that will produce consequences (karma) homosexuals will have to accept. Casual Christians tend to discourage it but admit that, even though it may not be their preference, theologically and in terms of their own values they can accept it if the relationship is a true expression of lasting love. Skeptics, of course, consider it a nonissue because it is a matter of private choice.

Diving into the worldview waters is important because it helps us to understand the challenges facing our nation and how Americans from divergent tribal viewpoints address each issue. As you can see from the preceding chapters regarding the beliefs and consequent behavior of each of the nation's faith tribes, each group sees the world differently because it interprets information and experiences through a different grid. Each tribe has the same context for consideration, but arrives at different conclusions from that same reality. This is because of the unique filter possessed by each tribe.

Note that the faith tribes not only interpret reality differently, they also respond to that reality in dissimilar ways. This is because we act on what we believe to be true or right. If we view something as appropriate, we respond one way; if we view it as inappropriate, we respond to it another way; if we see it as irrelevant, we respond differently yet again.

In light of the fundamental argument of this book—i.e., America is being torn apart by our failure to talk and work together toward a shared set of desired outcomes, based on a common set of values that we possess—getting a grip on the worldview dimension is crucial to developing a solution to the nation's existing dilemma.

WHO BELIEVES WHAT?

While it is possible to explain the dominant worldviews available to people, in reality you have probably never encountered anyone who completely embodied one of them. (For a brief synopsis of the dominant worldviews entertained by Americans, see appendix 1.) In fact, as you examine each tribe, you will observe several outcomes related to the worldviews of its members:

- First, there is no worldview that is universally held by everyone in any given tribe.
- Second, each tribal member possesses a worldview that reflects his or her personal acceptance of elements drawn from various worldviews—and even theological beliefs borrowed from other tribes.
- Third, very few individuals are able to articulate the elements of their worldviews. Even fewer can explain why they embrace the disparate pieces of their worldviews.
- Fourth, when confronted about the inconsistencies between their personal worldviews and the beliefs promoted by their tribes, people are generally unaware of such incompatibilities—and will also do nothing to rectify the conflicts.

All of this, of course, has contributed to the present cultural dynamic in which people do not know how to interact effectively with each other on matters of substance. They do not have the personal motivation or the analytic and dialogical tools to engage in a meaningful exchange on these matters.

Do not forget that the classic worldviews described in appendix 1 are theoretical constructs developed by scholars and philosophers. These intellectuals have endeavored to identify a set of ideas that are internally consistent and lead to predictable behaviors. Their efforts have provided us with psychologically and emotionally provocative ideas.

But in reality, *such worldviews are just straw dogs.* They do not exist in a pure form to any significant degree, if at all, in America. In fact, most people are unconcerned about philosophical issues such as truth and worldview. And they behave inconsistently— doing one thing that smacks of a secular humanist orientation and following it up with a behavior that reflects a Christian theist orientation and then another action that suggests a postmodern perspective. If you point out the inconsistencies to them, they shrug and move on without giving it a second thought.

Most Americans are not philosophers. We're survivors, entrepreneurs, pleasure seekers, adventurers, and even inveterate communicators. But few of us are deep, sophisticated, reflective thinkers. Books regarding philosophy and systemic analysis of our world sell poorly; exciting novels and self-help guides ring the cash register. Television programs that delve into intellectual waters regarding matters of science, theology, philosophy, or ethics get the dreaded Nielsen asterisk (an audience rating that means less than one percent of all television viewers tuned in to that show); but show a bunch of desperate housewives coping with suburban life or singers competing for a record deal and the ratings hit the roof. If you want to throw a well-received party, promise unlimited junk food and drinks along with a big event playing on the huge plasma screen; to clear a room quickly, invite guests to participate in a discussion of deistic moral foundations or the dangers of Western thought in an Arab culture.

We're not stupid; we just arrive at our conclusions through

more subconscious, nonconfrontational means. We know what we like when we see it, hear it, or feel it—and when we like something we embrace it, whether it is morally, theologically, philosophically, or intellectually compatible with our other choices or not.

It is this chaotic ambivalence toward perfect integration that makes our current situation in the United States so dangerous. In a negotiation, you act in light of the predictability of the opponent's position. But Americans are increasingly unpredictable—sometimes bordering on random—because we have so few interrelated moorings. It's hard to have a decent conversation about things that matter when your fellow conversationalist has facts and opinions but cannot tell the difference between them and has never taken the time to weave them into a larger concept of how his or her world works.

Americans harbor a patchwork of ideas that pass for their worldviews: it is wisdom by default and action based on impulse. You never know how people will react or for how long they will stand by their responses.

Leading such a group is treacherous. That's especially true within a democratic context, where people assume they should have freedom to make choices and their leaders should be responsive to their needs. Strategically charting a path to the future is challenging, to say the least.

SHARED VALUES EMERGE

Without the benefit of a carefully conceived worldview that serves as a reliable and consistent filter for interpreting reality and responding to situations, developing community is difficult.

The default mode, then, becomes reliance upon the shared values that the tribes possess. Delving into the core beliefs of each tribe provides a means of identifying the values we have in common. We can then use these shared principles as a foundation to build a genuine community of like-minded people. Leaders can develop and promote visions of the future that align with these values. The media can respect our need for unity and provide content that advances our understanding and pursuit of these values, rather than emphasizing discord and generating divisive controversy. Families can teach their children how to live in harmony with our shared principles. Individuals can realize their potential within the context of community by investing themselves in a life purpose that honors these values.

Let's consider what values we have in common.

America's Top Twenty: Our Shared Values

1. Represent the truth well
2. Develop inner peace and purity
3. Seek peace with others
4. Demonstrate wisdom
5. Be forgiving
6. Practice self-restraint
7. Get yourself together before criticizing
8. Invest in young people
9. Respect life
10. Treat others how you want to be treated
11. Be a good citizen
12. Justify people's respect
13. Avoid harmful behavior
14. Honor the elderly
15. Be generous
16. Do not judge or condemn others
17. Be mutually respectful of human rights
18. Cultivate civility
19. Belong to a caring community
20. Facilitate basic skills

Represent the truth well
While most of America's faith tribes contend that there are no moral absolutes and that truth is in the eye of the beholder, all of the tribes concur that consistently conveying truth, whatever a

person understands it to be, is appropriate. Intentionally leading people astray is rejected by each tribe as mutually detrimental. Honesty is still deemed to be the best policy.

Develop inner peace and purity

Inner peace results from the pursuit of qualities such as goodness, kindness, compassion, love, and gentleness. Some tribes consider these to be personal virtues while others perceive them to be marks of a spiritually transformed individual. Based on the notion that we cannot give what we don't have, the development of these qualities enables each of us to leave a positive imprint on the world—and to feel good about having done so.

Seek peace with others

Each day brings new challenges and tribulations. Those who seek to avoid hostility with other people effectively inject a degree of tranquillity and sanity into our chaotic and competitive world. Introducing peace into every interpersonal connection not only advances human survival but facilitates better communication and relationships.

Demonstrate wisdom

A wise person is revered because of various attributes: he or she is teachable, a good listener, and possesses patience, reflection, good judgment, common sense, curiosity, inner strength, contentment, humility, discipline, and appropriate fear. Wise people are reliable and live with greater joy.

Be forgiving

Some tribes promote forgiveness because they believe they have been granted forgiveness by God. Others push forgiveness as a means to ridding themselves of harmful thoughts, inner hostility, or other feelings that diminish their mental, physical, or spiritual health. In all tribes, though, having the strength and will to forgive is viewed as a virtue.

Practice self-restraint

Applying self-control and living within reasonable self-imposed boundaries are marks of a mature person. Those who can control themselves have a better chance of treating others with respect and civility.

Get yourself together before criticizing

A natural human tendency is to identify and criticize the faults in others without recognizing those same faults in ourselves. This is both hypocritical and counterproductive. If all of us focused on raising ourselves to a higher standard, we would be less interested in criticizing others.

Invest in young people

The most important qualities of a person are developed when he or she is young. As a human race, we have an obligation to prepare young people for a successful and meaningful future. This is both a privilege and a duty; the quality with which we carry out this task determines the quality of the future.

Respect life

Tribes differ on their views of life—whether it is a gift, an inevitability, an opportunity, or a consequence—but they concur that life is a resource to be respected.

Treat others how you want to be treated

The Golden Rule plays well across all the tribes as a fundamental principle. While this could be motivated by sheer self-interest, it is an ideal that people understand and accept as reasonable.

Be a good citizen

Regardless of one's faith, there is widespread appreciation for the freedoms and benefits of living in the United States. Cynicism and criticisms aside, Americans value their country and are open to doing what is necessary (albeit with some prodding) to ensure continuity of the country's greatness.

Justify people's respect

Everyone wants respect. Some do not understand the importance of earning it, believing that it should automatically be given, but there is no argument about the significance of being respected by others. Having respect is a major factor in personal dignity; being able to justify receiving respect is desirable.

Avoid harmful behavior

Although people sometimes lose their temper and may occasionally view violence as the only solution to their situation, even the most hostile individual usually recognizes the wisdom of not harming people. To distinguish us from animals or from evil people, drawing the line at hurtful behavior is almost universally embraced, both as a spiritual principle and as common sense.

Honor the elderly

For some tribes, blessing the elderly is a tradition, for others it is an example of indifference to age, and for others it is a way of paying the dues so that someday they will be appreciated and cared for in like manner. Several tribes teach that it is an adult child's duty to care for aged relatives; most tribes believe that older people have earned respect and care.

Be generous

A few tribes believe in reciprocity—that what you give is what you get. Others contend that generosity is a reflection of a grateful heart. Another tribe perceives generosity to be a means to building a better society. No matter what the motivation, Americans realize that giving is as good, if not better, than getting. They may define the parameters of generosity differently, but all tribes recognize it as a quality of greatness.

Do not judge or condemn others

While tolerance can quickly become a "politically correct" parody, all tribes promote the notion of allowing people to reap the natural consequences of their choices without any of us assuming the role of supreme judge. There is a distinction to be made between discernment and judgment, but making definitive judgments about the behavior of others is counterproductive for everyone. Those who believe in a Supreme Being should allow that spirit to judge; those who do not believe in a personal deity tend to believe that it is best to focus on our own behavior rather than on that of others.

Be mutually respectful of human rights

Life is valuable; if we did not believe this, we would not have children and we would not seek to live long lives. While there may be extraordinary situations in which a life may be taken, those are exceptions. Apart from those infrequent times, people deserve to be treated with dignity and respect.

Cultivate civility

Be courteous and polite. There is no excuse for rude behavior. A society that fosters vulgarity in any form is a culture in descent. Each tribe has its own motivation for encouraging civility, ranging from demonstrating love to protecting one's physical security and reputation.

Belong to a caring community

One of the basic human instincts is to belong to a group that provides acceptance and basic needs (e.g., food, shelter, safety). No tribe preaches living in isolation; meaningful interaction with other people provides the emotional stability each of us needs.

Facilitate basic skills

Every tribe wants its people to be prepared to succeed in the material world, if only at a basic level. To enable success, people must master basic skills—such as literacy, hygiene, reflective thinking, interpersonal abilities, and vocational preparation.

THE PATH FORWARD

As you read through the list of values, you probably resonated with most if not all of them. *This is a no-brainer*, you might be thinking, *pretty much everyone buys into these values. But America has bought into them for decades—and yet we're in a big mess. How could something we've embraced for so long be the key to resurrecting our future?*

It's a reasonable question. In essence, the United States is suffering from the loss of good character. It is widely assumed that our public officials lie to us. Millions of frivolous lawsuits are entered into each year as a means of intimidating people or manipulating situations to force a desired, if undeserved, outcome. Numerous employees cut corners on the job, either putting in for extra time they don't deserve or taking home company materials for personal use. The alcoholic beverage industry generates tens of billions of dollars in revenue because millions of Americans get plastered each week. One of the most common forms of communication is gossip. More of us feel compassion toward the people suffering in the world than do anything substantive about it. Our loyalty extends only as far as the last benefit we received from those who desire our support. We deem hard times to be a curse rather than a gift. And the list goes on and on.

Faith, when appropriately applied, builds strong character. Sadly, the nation's faith has been overshadowed by other pursuits and preferences that have minimized the importance of the beliefs and worldview that build true character. So we need a plan for restoration.

The key building block for the restoration of America is a return to—and emphasis upon—the character qualities that make a nation great. Without the advantage of a full-blown, carefully developed worldview that we can agree upon as the basis for positive behavior, the fallback strategy is to rely upon the accumulation of a series of worldview components that can be joined together to lead us to more comprehensive and beneficial ways of thinking about and responding to life.

That's where our core values come in: they are those individual signposts that can help us find our way back to moral, spiritual, emotional, and intellectual health. America lost its way on the journey to cultural maturity, but accentuating our shared values can get us back on the right road again. Those shared values are the remnant of a mind-set that once made us great. With proper guidance and commitment, they can rescue us from the destructive path we are on today.

If you still wonder what this would look like, envision a society in which our leaders continually guide us toward the fulfillment of visions that depend upon people exhibiting such values.

Imagine a media environment in which the objective is not to build an audience through controversy and division, but by lifting up the good and positive elements of our nation and its potential.

Think what it would be like if families accepted the challenge to raise up cultural champions—children who learned their spiritual and moral foundations at home and then had those views and behaviors reinforced in the marketplace. Instead of allowing worldview-by-default to be our dominant process, our young people would receive character education that could enable them to be dynamic world citizens rather than selfish and cynical capitalists. (Understand: I am *not* against capitalism. I am, however, appalled by the manipulation, dishonesty, injustice, and avarice that have come to characterize the way we now deploy the capitalist process.)

Dream with me about a future in which every citizen fills a meaningful role in a world-class democracy, contributing value to the expansion of all dimensions of the nation. This need not be "pie in the sky idealism," as some have rebuked it; it simply takes a different kind of leader and a very different kind of follower—both committed to the same outcomes in the same way that an oncologist and her cancer patient are determined to work in concert to defeat the disease that threatens the patient.

What could possibly defeat a nation knit together by honesty, mutual respect, generosity, and civility? A country filled with people characterized by inner peace and strength, self-restraint, grace, and wisdom would be unstoppable. Think about the potential America would have if its people were turned loose to invest in young people, model compassionate servanthood, and develop a national network of caring communities.

Isn't that what you would want to experience? If you could drop your guard for a moment and allow yourself to visualize our best scenario, wouldn't it look like that?

How does that get translated into the daily grind of the average Casual Christian, Mormon, or Pantheist? From the time we wake up to when our heads hit the pillow at night, our life orientation would be challenged. Our everyday experiences would be transformed, because we

- would not accept dishonesty from politicians but would instead call them out on the absurd or unjustifiably expensive programs and policies they advocate;
- would refuse to buy products from companies that twist the minds and hearts of our children through manipulative advertising and unsubstantiated product claims;
- would purposefully use fewer words during the course of our day because we would refuse to engage in gossip, half-truths, or deceptive speech;
- would conscientiously limit our spending to those material goods that we need and a few conveniences that we could easily afford, without racking up any debt;
- would studiously avoid situations in which we would be tempted to sexually or emotionally compromise our relationships with our spouses or our moral commitments to our children and friends;
- would gracefully extend forgiveness to those who have hurt us, after having honest confrontations with them over the pain they caused;
- would identify one or more young people, other than our own children or grandchildren, in whom we could invest our time and expertise, encouraging them to mature more fully;

- would grieve the loss of life experienced by other families, whether it be through engagement in wartime activities, street-level hostilities, natural disasters, or death wrought by aging or illness;
- would experience the joy of other people's celebratory moments: a new birth, a wedding, a superior job performance;
- would not tolerate the abuse of another person's fundamental rights or dignity by individuals, organizations, or government;
- would refuse to respond to inappropriate speech directed toward us with similarly inappropriate speech or feelings.

This list is, of course, incomplete. Simply return to the shared values of our culture and apply each to your daily circumstances, and you will be able to fill in the gaps. And if you feel as if the list is a profile of deeds right out of a fairy tale, that may simply indicate that you have strayed further than you know from the fundamental precepts of your faith tribe and your nation.

These kinds of outcomes—these ways of life—are not easily achieved, but they are not far-fetched either. We could see this happen in our lifetimes if we were truly and fully committed to it. America is a can-do nation. We have pulled off countless miracles against the odds—but only when we really, intensely, passionately wanted it.

Do you want the United States to be great again, badly enough to do what it takes?

For this kind of rebirth of America, we will need each tribe to be part of the solution. No tribe would have to abandon its central beliefs or compromise its core doctrine in order to be a player in this revolution. If we can focus on shared, life-giving values such as those described above, we can become a united team and radically reshape this decaying, divided country. And if we refuse to do so, then we may very well be signing the nation's death certificate.

It is a democracy. The majority will choose. But the majority is made up of an accumulation of individuals who make choices. What will you choose for our future?

CHAPTER

TEN

Empowering Values-
Driven Leaders

PEOPLE often see themselves differently than others do. A great example of this is the fact that more than six out of every ten Americans consider themselves to be leaders. Yet when you explore what it means to lead and compare that to the activities and attitudes of those people, you quickly discover that the self-perception of tens of millions of people is off base. They are not so much lying as they are innocently ignorant about what leadership is and who they really are.

For what it's worth, our extensive research regarding a full range of factors related to leadership suggests that perhaps one out of every seven Americans is a leader. But whatever the true percentage is, one fact is indisputable: every American is, to a considerable degree, a follower.

Think about it. People whose jobs demand leadership have to occasionally follow the direction and rely upon the guidance of other people in order to facilitate their own leadership needs and desired outcomes. Even the president of the United States, often described as the most powerful leader in the world, constantly switches back and forth between the leader and follower roles. The president must work with Congress, state and local officials, federal bureaucrats, lobbying groups, the media, voter coalitions, and more—all of which at times temporarily take the baton and direct the flow of communication and activity. How well the president operates as a follower in those moments significantly influences his ability to lead effectively when he takes back the baton to move forward on his own agenda. That same principle is true for every leader.

In a democracy, leadership is not seized or inherited; it is granted by the people to chosen individuals. If there is a paucity of effective leadership, as I suggest we suffer from today, it is not because the nation lacks men and women sufficiently gifted as leaders but because the followers who empower individuals to lead have made bad choices.

What we wind up with is a glut of people who market themselves as leaders but lack what it takes to be effective leaders. These false leaders are able to persuade followers to hand them the baton because most of us have no idea what we are searching for in a leader. We choose on the basis of how we feel about a person, how well he or she projects on camera and how humorous, pleasant, or articulate that person seems to be. As a consequence, we empower individuals who do not have what it takes to advance society in ways that fit with our values.

Whom we select to serve as our leaders, and the basis on which we choose them, is of paramount importance. Although followers bear the responsibility for choosing individuals to lead us forward, it is the task of those leaders to define reality for us. They provide the context for interpretation and a vision for the future, as well as the permission, encouragement, guidance, and resources to pursue that ideal.

So one of your chief responsibilities as an American citizen is to become the best follower you can be. Your performance as a follower determines how capably others can lead: after all, vision without execution is just an interesting idea. It is in the accomplishment of a vision founded upon our shared values that leaders and followers are able to work together to improve the human condition.

Every one of us has a responsibility to carry our own weight in the renewal of our society. We take cues from our leaders, but we have the obligation of doing our part in the restoration process. A leader who conveys an appropriate and compelling vision that people fail to enact has not really led anyone; he or she has simply filled the air with words, produced discouragement or dissatisfaction, and consumed valuable resources. Great leaders work with people to produce specific results that convert vision to reality. But no leader sees the vision flourish unless followers get the job done.

America's restoration depends largely on the quality of followership that you and I and our fellow citizens provide.

What can we, the people, do to become better followers? Until we do so, we cannot expect superior leadership to emerge. At this juncture in America's history, the burden of improvement is on our shoulders. What steps can we take to transfer a greater portion of that burden to the shoulders of our leaders, so that it becomes a shared responsibility? How can we enhance our performance as followers in ways that help restore America to a position of strength and growth?

TWELVE COMMITMENTS OF GREAT FOLLOWERS

Drawing on the research we regularly conduct regarding leadership and followership, let me offer the following observations about what it takes to be an effective follower. My suggestion is that every one of us conduct a personal evaluation of how well we are performing these tasks and identify ways in which we can become more efficient in their implementation.

For the sake of identification, let's refer to these as the Twelve Commitments of Great Followers.

Commitment 1: Know what you're looking for in a leader

First, we must be clear about what we are looking for in a leader. Too often we get distracted by charisma, momentum, or other peripheral factors.

The best leaders are those who are passionate about guiding

people toward a vision to which they will commit their lives. That vision needs to be a compelling description of a preferable future, based on our common values, that we can work together to achieve. Unless such a vision is front and center in the mind, heart, and efforts of someone who seeks our support, that person is not deserving of our support.

Vision is the air that leaders breathe; it is their currency. Different leaders will offer divergent visions for our consideration. We must be certain that the recommended visions coincide with our values and are a portrait of a future condition that we are willing to pursue with vigor.

Those who seek our support must also possess certain qualities that show us they have what it takes to help us improve the world. In addition to an unshakable commitment to leading us toward the vision, we need leaders who have outstanding character (e.g., honesty, modesty, compassion, consistency, justness, trustworthiness, loyalty, and diligence). How could we confidently partner with a leader who lacks such traits?

And, of course, as we screen possible leaders we must be sure that they have what it takes to get the job done in terms of skills. Leaders are responsible for motivating, directing, and mobilizing people to pursue the vision, while ensuring that sufficient resources are available to get the job done. No individual has all the skills and talents required to facilitate visionary change, so our best leaders must also be great team players, able to work well with other leaders whose gifts and abilities supplement and complement their own.

So when it comes down to it, selecting leaders is more involved than just feeling good about someone who wants to lead. When we buy a house, we do our homework to make sure that everything we have been told is accurate and that we are getting what we think we're getting. When our children choose a college to attend, we beat the bushes for information about the school, talking to school officials, current students, graduates, and employers to discern the truth about the school. We need to take the selection of our leaders every bit as seriously. These choices have a dramatic effect on our lives.

Commitment 2: Live and die for the vision

Our future is determined by the vision to which our leaders are guiding us. That means our first duty as followers is to be sure we know what we are signing up for. Leadership is not just about the person who serves as the leader; it's just as focused on the vision the leader will promote. If we like a leader but are not too crazy about the vision he or she represents, that in and of itself is grounds for abandoning that leader.

Similarly, leaders can get distracted by all the demands of the job. They frequently lose sight of the vision and get immersed in administrative or other details that sidetrack the entire enterprise. As a follower, you have an obligation to insist that the leader stay focused on the vision, keep followers focused on the vision, and never veer from pursuing the core of the vision.

As a follower, it is not your job to develop the vision. But it is your job to select leaders based on the vision they promote and then devote yourself to the implementation of that outcome.

Practically speaking, what do you do if a leader comes to power who promotes a vision you do not endorse? As a citizen, you have the right to critique the vision, but you also have a duty to support it. You are not free to undermine the entire community because it chose a direction you do not affirm. You can certainly disagree and express your preference, but you must also do your best to support the community in its pursuit of its chosen vision. Your alternative, of course, is to leave that community and join another.

One of the reasons America has struggled in the past quarter century is that so many people have decided that they don't like the direction things are going and simply disengage. They stop paying taxes, voting, dialoguing, and serving. They become a drain on the entire community, even though they derive benefit from it. That is the essence of bad followership. Our system has mechanisms that facilitate the expression of appropriate disapproval. Working outside the system, even through seemingly innocuous means such as disrespectful blog content, rude public comments, knowingly deceitful allegations about a leader or conditions—these and similar activities conflict with our core values and injure the community.

Commitment 3: Refuse to settle for anything but the best

The consumer axiom "You get what you pay for" can easily be adapted to the way we follow leaders: the quality of our leaders determines the quality of our lives.

Some of my friends are very blasé about the selection of leaders, figuring their participation doesn't make any difference. For a few of them, this reflects their deterministic worldview: the "what will be, will be" mentality. Others assume that all leaders can be molded by pressure once they assume their position. Those are dangerous and costly perspectives.

If you embrace mediocrity from the start, you can expect nothing less than mediocrity throughout the process. Settling for anything less than the best disrespects you and your community; it reflects low self-esteem, as if you're not worthy of anything better. Accepting subpar leadership sets you up for disappointment, if not failure.

The beauty of a democracy is that you have the ability to create the best possible future through your spirited participation in the process. Why settle for inferiority when better alternatives are yours for the asking?

Getting quality leaders might take some effort on your part—offering encouragement or other inducements—but provides a synergistic outcome: you have served both your own interests and those of the community. When you find men and women of passion, character, and competence who reflect your values and represent a compelling vision, backing them promises a good return on your investment. In a nation as diverse as ours, there is an ample pool of talent to draw from; you must have the discernment and determination to intelligently pick those leaders whom you can get excited about following.

Commitment 4: Provide constructive feedback

Every freedom brings responsibilities with it. Americans constantly exercise freedom of speech, but sometimes we don't give much thought to the power and effect of the words we speak so freely. Most faith traditions underscore the importance of using speech to build up rather than tear down. And that's how we can best use our words, as followers, when we deal with leaders.

Leadership is a very difficult task, even for those who are innately gifted to lead. One of the best gifts we can bring to the party is constructive feedback. When we interact with leaders, our job is to express appreciation for their work, encourage them to continue and to do their best, and to provide constructive criticism if any is necessary. It is not our job—nor in anyone's best interest—to offer destructive remarks.

For that matter, our conversations with fellow followers should rise to the same standard: speak positively and kindly, seeking to promote favorable outcomes. Before speaking, it is important to consider the effects of what we wish to say and how we plan to say it. On many occasions, silence is the best option. The world does not always need to hear our opinions, no matter how interesting or right they may seem to us.

Constructive comments, on the other hand, add value to the situation. If our intent is to provide uplifting, helpful insight without injuring anyone, we have an obligation to speak up. If our words are likely to cause harm or division, though, we are best advised to hold our tongues.

Paradoxically, leaders serve followers. Followers need to keep leaders on track as much as leaders need to guide followers in the pursuit of the vision. We are all on the same team and must keep our eyes on the goal. Demand what is rightfully yours: leaders whose character and competencies are focused on empowering all of us to achieve the vision we have agreed to pursue. The only

THE SEVEN FAITH TRIBES / GEORGE BARNA

accountability that leaders will experience comes from you; take that privilege seriously.

Commitment 5: Hold leaders to the highest reasonable standards—and expect them to do the same with you

Leaders are supposed to elevate the life of followers on their joint pursuit of the vision. Toward that end, you want to search for leaders who can live up to a high standard—the same kind of moral, ethical, and productivity standards that you are willing to rise to. It's inappropriate for you to hold a leader to a standard that you refuse to live by. At the same time, it's fruitful for a leader to push you to raise your game to its highest level. That's the kind of leader you need to seek and support: one who will continue to rise above mediocrity and who wants to help you do the same.

The job of effective leaders is to create a better future, which can only be done if they are dissatisfied with the way things are. Hope springs from the belief that the future will be better than the present. People with power and influence who are content to maintain the status quo are not leaders worth investing your time and energy into. But unless there is some degree of accountability, many people are willing to do as little as possible to get by. Your job, as a follower, is to seek out leaders who offer a compelling vision (which implies improvement) and then to work with them to achieve it, holding them accountable en route.

Commitment 6: Always place community interest above self-interest

The current national malaise is partly attributable to the fact that so many Americans place their self-interest before common interest. In the end, this is a self-defeating strategy, both personally and nationally. The darker side of your human nature will draw you to "look out for number one." Do the math: if everyone just took care of his or her own needs, you would get—well, pretty much what we increasingly have in the United States today, which is the crux of our national problem. Selfishness is a choice. There are alternatives. Only you can determine what you will choose—and know that your choices define who you are and the world you will live in. One of the core values all of our tribes embrace is the notion behind the Golden Rule, that if we treat others as we want to be treated, a different tenor will permeate our existence, and we will experience more pleasant and positive outcomes. The world becomes a better place through our willingness to sacrifice for the common good.

The flip side of the selfishness coin is selflessness. This is what six of the seven faith tribes promote: living beyond yourself, becoming a laudable global citizen. Greatness always demands sacrifice, whether it is the greatness of a nation, a community, a company, a family, or an individual. To be a great follower, you must make up your mind that you will *not* grab for all the gusto and possibilities that exist; gluttony is not a virtue. Serving others through your willingness to forgo some possessions and pleasures in order to accomplish a greater good is a hallmark of respectable character—and a great citizen.

As a follower, this means you are wise to throw your full support behind those leaders who are driving you to achieve the greatest good. How can you support them? Listen to their guidance, obey their exhortations, pray for their wisdom and strength, and hold them accountable to make the vision a reality. If you do anything less, you have let down society and robbed yourself of the best you could be.

Commitment 7: Be proud of your leaders

Have you ever watched parents cheering for their children in an athletic event or other competition? It's moving to see the love they have for their sons or daughters. They don't care who knows it; they are going to support their children. They are proud to be their parents, and they are proud of the accomplishments and abilities of their young ones.

A nation becomes great when its people exude pride for their country and its leaders. A tribe has its greatest influence when it is proud of its leaders and their faith. A family optimizes its life when each member is proud of the others and is willing to do whatever he or she can to be supportive. A corporation excels when its executives and employees are proud of what they stand for, what they produce, and how they have blended together as an organization. A school is in its prime when it knows that it is living in concert with its purpose and values, and that its leaders are energizing the community to fulfill its potential.

How much pride do you have in your leaders and what they stand for? Until you are full-bore proud of them, something important is missing in your life and that of the community in question. If you lack that kind of smile-producing, warmhearted satisfaction, is it because you have the wrong leaders? Is it because you and other followers are failing to put out 100 percent?

Your attitude goes a long way toward determining both how you see the world and how you affect it. Don't underestimate your power to influence the world. You cannot change the entire world in a single day, but you can change one person or one situation, or influence one leader, today. And you can do it again tomorrow and the day after that. Yes, your schedule is packed with activities designed to help you survive another day. But you have what it takes to impact a small corner of the world. If you do your part, and every other follower does his or hers, imagine what we can accomplish together, moving in tandem toward the same vision for the same common good, based on our shared values!

America was built on a population of people who worked hard, had great expectations, and looked to their leaders to bring them to the pinnacle of performance. And they were willing to do their share in raising the bar. What about today? It's easier to complain and find fault than to dig deep and right the wrongs. Are you proud of your leaders? your country? your tribe? your family? your community? Who do you think will make matters even better, if not you?

Commitment 8: Become a great team player

The only way to experience a life that transcends mere survival is by diligently working as a team member. A team always out-performs an individual—and a team excels when it has complete commitment to a common goal.

No leader has ever single-handedly changed the world. Martin Luther King worked with a group of talented, single-minded col-leagues to enable the civil rights movement to progress. Ronald Reagan was the front man of a team of committed and strategic leaders who changed the world during his administration. Billy Graham was an effective evangelist whose efforts succeeded because of an army of people working together behind the scenes. Magic Johnson was the charismatic and talented force behind the world championships won by the Los Angeles Lakers, but he could not have done it without the coaching of Pat Riley and the comple-mentary skills of his teammates. Bill Gates is one of the wealthi-est people on earth and is well-known as the founder of Microsoft, but his vision was executed by an anonymous group of diligent and devoted coworkers (who are also enormously wealthy today).

All great leaders rely on the efforts of other leaders to com-plete the tasks they set for themselves. They recognize that the vision is bigger than they are able to accomplish on their own; they depend on the abilities and commitment of other leaders who can lead in ways they cannot. As you identify the leaders to whom you will entrust your future, ask yourself if they've surrounded themselves with a good team of leaders. Do other leaders line up to partner with them, or do they shy away from them? Also, are your leaders in it for themselves or for you?

Followers can be measured by the same criteria. As you exam-ine how you add value to the process, would you say it is through sheer hard work in isolation, or have you blended your talents and resources with those of other followers to serve in a com-munity environment?

One of the most accurate and helpful sayings I've heard is "It's amazing how much you can accomplish if you don't care who gets the credit." That's the mark of a great team player: staying focused on the goal, taking direction from the leader, and pouring your heart and soul into being the best teammate you can be. Know your role, understand its necessity if the team is to succeed, and be a good teammate—encouraging, supporting, pulling your weight, and reaping joy from the team's accomplishments and disappointment from the team's failures.

Commitment 9: Perform your duties with excellence

Great outcomes are the result of great effort. Naturally, you want to follow a leader who is going to produce outstanding results. But those results depend largely on what you invest in the process. Great results require that you always maximize your performance. When you and other followers generate superior productivity—high quantity, high quality—you make the leader look good. And that's your job: operate at such a lofty level of output that everyone emerges a winner.

If you take a careful look at the shared values of the nation, you'll see that an underlying thread is that we are meant to do our best, all the time. Sure, we get tired and complacent sometimes, but a good leader will call us back to a higher standard, and a good follower will heed the call. Remember, it's a partnership where you have given the leader the right to push you to a higher level, and you reserve the right to demand better guidance from the leader. When you perform your duties with excellence, it pushes the leader to raise his or her level too.

When it is time to choose a leader, opt for the one who is always striving for better results. Don't be seduced by those who think their track records have earned them the right to coast into the future.

And take a look in the mirror every once in a while to see how much you're pushing yourself to do your best. What you bring to the table matters—for your community as well as your self-respect. Every time you let up and produce subpar results, you have cheated yourself—and everyone else. Take pride in your work; show the world who you are and that a quality person produces quality output. Hardships and complexities will inevitably come your way, but they are never an excuse to give up or to do shoddy work.

Commitment 10: Add value all the time

Always add more value than you subtract. Imagine what would happen if the majority of people in our nation were committed to depositing more value into their communities than they withdrew. That's one of the reasons why America became great—and that's what it will take for us to return to greatness. Reap the satisfaction of knowing that you have invested in the future for your children and others. Feel the pleasure of recognizing that you have done your part in restoring the nation's strength. Continue to seek ways in which you are part of the solution.

Some followers think that showing up is good enough. It's not. Part of the challenge facing Americans today—in our places of business, our churches and places of worship, our schools, our halls of government, even in our living rooms—is for us to avoid settling for mere presence. Our responsibility to each other is to look for new ways to add value to the situation.

Leaders have a mandate to inspire us to seek out these opportunities and to aggressively pursue them. Followers have a mandate to own the vision and expand it in ways that are unique to their own gifts and experiences. That means being available—intellectually, emotionally, and physically—to push the limits. That means using your creative capacity to lift the vision to new levels. Ask yourself how you have added unexpected benefit to the community of which you are a part. Only by pushing yourself to take risks and investing more of yourself—along with a similar commitment by other followers—can we expect to make significant headway toward the vision.

Commitment 11: Focus on the future

Great leaders appreciate the past, live in the present, and think in the future. The same could be said of effective followers. If progress is to be made, it's neither realized by obsessing on nostalgic memories or trying to return to the old days, nor by settling in to produce more of the current reality. Leaders work with us to create the future. We can learn from the past and enjoy the present, but our real challenge is to make the most of the days to come. Are you working with a leader who has that perspective and zeal? Are you supporting your leaders to make the dream come true?

To get the most from the future, we must prepare for it today. That challenges us to constantly develop new leaders, not only to help out today but also so that younger or less experienced leaders will be available to meet the growing and unique demands of the future. As a support person in the leader's army, be sure to recognize that you help to train and prepare tomorrow's leaders. Doing so draws on some of our shared values, such as showing self-restraint, demonstrating understanding and patience toward others, investing in other people (especially young people who are maturing into their value-producing roles), respecting others, and demonstrating what it means to be part of a caring and nurturing community.

It is good for followers to cultivate a desire to participate in the development of the future. This mind-set causes us to benignly exploit the opportunities we have for enhancing our quality of life in the future. Focus your attention and energy on how to be part of a team that is building a better world, not for personal gain as much as for the advantage of the entire community. Remember, when the community wins, you win; when you win, your leaders win.

Commitment 12: Keep growing personally
Every living thing has two choices: grow or die. If you're not doing one, you are doing the other. My advice: choose growth!

Pushing yourself beyond where you are opens up new possibilities—for you and for everyone else. Life becomes stale when you deem yourself to be fully mature. If history teaches us anything, it is that we can accomplish much more than we ever imagined—and that it is much harder than we might have hoped. But that's what distinguishes the great nations from the also-rans: people in the memorable civilizations never stop growing.

Another lesson you can draw from your predecessors is that when you think you know it all, you have just lost the heartbeat of life. Growth is about discovery and experience. The more experiences you have that facilitate understanding and wisdom, the better equipped you are to prosper the world. Joy and excitement are found in growing deep. In contrast, those who cease to push the boundaries of knowledge and wisdom merely experience entropy.

What can you do to grow? Return to the shared values, and set new and realistic goals for yourself in relation to each one. Cultivating civility might see you move along a continuum from stopping rude comments all the way to serving as a peacemaker in other relationships. Becoming a generous person might bring you from saying kind things to people at one end of the scale to donating 20 percent of your income to the needy at the other end. Developing courtesy might mean you start out working at being a kind and respectful individual to eventually becoming one of the most fulfilled and consistent servants of others in your midst.

The Twelve Commitments of Great Followers

Commitment 1: Know what you're looking for in a leader
Commitment 2: Live and die for the vision
Commitment 3: Refuse to settle for anything but the best
Commitment 4: Provide constructive feedback
Commitment 5: Hold leaders to the highest reasonable standards—and expect them to do the same with you
Commitment 6: Always place community interest above self-interest
Commitment 7: Be proud of your leaders
Commitment 8: Become a great team player
Commitment 9: Perform your duties with excellence
Commitment 10: Add value all the time
Commitment 11: Focus on the future
Commitment 12: Keep growing personally

Stretch past the limits you or others have set for yourself. It's a win-win situation.

EXAMINING THE LEADERS YOU ARE FOLLOWING

As noted earlier in this book, America is at a pivotal point today. We need leaders who will heal and grow America. You have tremendous power because you get to select which leaders you will grant the privilege of leading you. Support those who call us to a higher standard, whose vision is to restore the country's greatness by bringing people together and rebuilding an American community founded on mutual respect, shared values, kindness and generosity, compassion for those in need, and effective communication.

Be forewarned: choosing great leaders is tricky. You will encounter would-be leaders who will try to seduce you with displays of charisma, clever talk, comforting ideas, and creative concepts. Those are dangerous distractions. Stay focused on the end goal: working in partnership with visionary leaders who count on you to be a contributor to national greatness through our joint commitment to appropriate visions and a body of shared values. Do what you can to be sure that the visions you come to own are mutually compatible; endorsing visions that essentially work against each other undermines everything you invest in the process.

TRIBES NEED GREAT LEADERS AND FOLLOWERS

One of the oddities about the faith tribes of America is that they seem distracted from their primary purpose. Rather than pursuing a vision of moving people toward excellence, they often get bogged down in administrative and logistic activity. None of the tribes has been called to focus upon constructing more buildings, hiring more professionals, developing extensive programs, or even attracting record numbers of people to their events and membership rolls. Given the values that each tribe represents, a central purpose of their existence is to help people become better human beings. For some of the tribes (like the Captive Christians), that is a by-product of their primary objective (i.e., getting right with God), while for others it is an end in itself.

To help their people's lives reflect the values their tribe embraces, great leaders are required to help followers focus on what truly matters. Many people have a tendency to think of leadership in terms of government and business. However, each tribe needs numerous superb leaders to guide people on a journey of dynamic growth.

As you consider your tribe, what kind of leaders do you have who communicate a vision that reflects the fundamental principles, values, and objectives of your faith? Are they caught up in the day-to-day trivialities of organizational life, or do they help you stay focused on the things that ultimately matter? Your obligation as a follower is not merely to do what you're told, but to know what you believe and why you believe it, and to align yourself with tribal leaders who empower you to continually grow in your faith.

Many tribes liken their adherents to sheep who must know and follow the voice of their master. That is a common metaphor in the theology of the Christian, Jewish, and Mormon tribes. A useful insight about sheep, though, is that they only follow the voice of a shepherd with whom they feel comfortable—that is, one whom they have grown to know over time and whom they perceive to be looking out for their best interests. They are merely following their most basic instinct: the need to survive. As such, you, too, need to follow shepherds (i.e., leaders) who have your best interests in mind—hopefully shepherds who can help you transcend mere survival and enable you to achieve the more fulfilling possibilities of life as a believer.

Don't overlook the way your faith enables you to become a great follower (or leader). It provides you with the motivation and the means to become a person who embodies the shared values that are the foundation of a great nation and a better life. It offers a community in which you can grow into that lifestyle. And your tribe represents the safe harbor from which you can launch out as a person who can change the world by being who you are meant to be. Lean on your tribe for strength, wisdom, and encouragement. That's what a family of faith provides to its members.

IF YOU ARE A HABITUAL LEADER

Having read through this chapter, you might appreciate the clarification of what it means to be a great follower, but you might be frustrated if you are also a genuine leader. (Through our research we have learned it is important to distinguish between the leadership that everyone has to provide in certain situations from the leadership demanded of people whose primary talent and focus in life is leading others. We refer to the former as "situational leaders" and the latter as "habitual leaders.") What about leadership principles and guidance? What do you need to know?

I'd encourage you simply to consider the needs of followers that are outlined above and convert those into a self-evaluation process and subsequent action plan for you as a habitual leader. For instance, if followers need to own and pursue a vision for the future, it is your job to envision, communicate, and mobilize people around such a vision. If it is important for followers to take pride in their leaders, then you must live and lead in a way that gives them ample reason to be proud to be on your team. If followers are supposed to add value to the cause, then you must be sensitive to their efforts to do so and provide opportunities for them to expose their ideas and be honored for their efforts to advance the cause.

Ultimately, if you have the passion and gifts to lead, the character to model the shared values, and the competencies to get things done, then you have the raw qualifications to lead.[26] But until you work with a team of leaders, coalesced around a compelling vision, and are able to motivate, mobilize, supply, and direct people in the pursuit of that vision, you're not really leading. When you are able to implement such efforts, you are adding tremendous value to the community and making the most of your talents and opportunities in life.

WHETHER YOU LEAD OR FOLLOW
Keep this in mind: life is short and difficult, but you can enjoy the ride. While the worldview of each tribe has a different spin on our experience of eternity, each one agrees that there is value in living in the moment and enjoying it for what it is. Life has purpose. You will only reap the benefit of that purpose when you allow yourself to grow from each experience and see your life as a wonderful adventure. Don't accept the burden of responsibility for everyone's experience. Make your contribution and accept each new day as a gift to be savored.

CHAPTER
ELEVEN
Recommissioning the Media

EFFECTIVE visionary leadership can move America closer to health, but every leader needs a broad base of support to achieve his or her goals. One indispensable support item is committed followers. In our current cultural context an equally significant source of support is the media.

While the media may seem like wallpaper to some people—that is, it's unobtrusively ubiquitous—we must be careful not to overlook the incredible influence the media have upon our society. Every leader communicates vision within a cultural context. That context is largely defined in people's minds by the media.

Several years ago I led a research project in which we evaluated the relative impact of different sources of influence on people's lives in the United States. The outcome was stunning. In brief, we discovered that there are three distinct levels of impact. The top tier of influence entities includes family; public policies; and five forms of media: movies, television, music, the Internet, and books. We discovered that an estimated 60 percent to 70 percent of a typical person's worldview and resulting behavior have been significantly shaped by the information and experience received from those seven sources. The middle tier of influence consists of about a dozen different entities, such as schools, peers, athletes, and several more media forms (radio, video games, newspapers, and magazines). That tier appeared to have 20 percent to 30 percent of the influence upon a typical person's life decisions. The bottom tier, which usually has about 10 percent of the influence on a person's choices, consisted of nearly two dozen entities, including churches.

The project revealed several important insights. First, each of us is affected by a wide range of external influences—none of which is dominant among all people. Second, when we compared what people credited as having influenced them and what actually had influenced them, we realized that much of the impact we experience goes undetected and unacknowledged, as the gap between those profiles made it clear. Third, the media have become dangerously influential—and largely unaccountable for their influence.

Some people have argued that the greatest value of this research was the relative ranking or specific percentages of influence exerted by the various entities. However, the true value of the study was providing a map of the contours of influence in America. In essence, the data showed that we are typically impacted primarily by three major sources of input: family, media, and government. Each of those sources builds on the other, and the influence of each is affected by that of the others as well. And because of the extensive reach of each of those entities, the mind and heart of every one of us are shaped in some measure by that trio of trainers.

THE FEAR OF CENSORSHIP

Some who are reading this—perhaps you are among them—might be squirming right now, uneasy with this train of reasoning, fearing that I am leading to a call for ideology-based limitations to be imposed on media content. Many Americans are scared that censorship might occur. These champions of the First Amendment to our Constitution would rather die fighting for the capacity to freely express whatever they choose than to succumb to the reduction, much less elimination, of that right.

Relax! I am not suggesting the imposition of media censorship. I believe if people truly understand what is at stake and how they can be part of the solution to the restoration of America's stature, there is no need to entertain such ideas. In a society undermined by its own selfish nature, recovery begins by addressing self-interest: the likely loss of freedom, comfort, opportunity, and hope that will inevitably occur if we continue to make the choices that are dismantling our nation. In a sense, our desire for healthy survival ranks higher than our stubborn desire to ensure that any content is available anywhere via any means.

American history documents a long trail of citizens who chose to see the big picture—the glorious freedoms we have and the hard work and sacrifice it takes to maintain them—and who consequently made appropriate choices designed to support the unique strength of our democracy. Imposing limitations should not be necessary. If we all agree that freedom is the result of citizens embracing both the rights and responsibilities offered in our founding documents and being willing to make personal sacrifices for the good of the national community, then there will be no need to force such restrictions. People will voluntarily incorporate necessary changes into their everyday lives. These should be self-imposed limitations that lead to cultural health and individual well-being.

The Bible even speaks to this issue when it instructs us that all things that are permissible are not necessarily profitable for us.[27] That's precisely the choice that lies in front of Americans regarding media content. Legally, we have the right to do things that morally and relationally corrupt us—by the standards of all the tribes.

Inviting people to deliver what the nation needs in order to protect and perpetuate our freedom is a tactic with abundant precedent. But before we get to that stage of the discussion, let's examine how the media fit within our society today.

THE PLACE OF MEDIA IN AMERICAN LIFE

The United States has become a media-rich society. It is hard to go anywhere without being exposed to some form of media—and even harder to remember or imagine what life was like before the ubiquity of the Internet, iPods, DVDs, and the rest. But the omnipresence of these tools raises an important question: why are the media so influential?

Perhaps our culture has become media saturated because each form of media is a composite—that is, an input that typically combines and integrates the contributions of people, information, and sensory stimulation into a memorable experience that affects our views of and responses to life.

Over the years, as technological breakthroughs have overcome delivery and capacity limitations, the media have become more prolific in our lives. The progression of forms during the past century—from print (books, newspaper, magazines) to broadcast (radio, television) to digital (Internet, MP3s, MPEGs)—has completely altered the way we experience reality. The encroachment of these media has impacted us in numerous ways:

- **Schedules:** Our daily agendas dedicate generous amounts of time to media exposure. Making sure that we optimize our schedules without losing out on desired media options has challenged us to balance real-time media and time shifting.
- **Relationships:** Our connections with people are influenced by how often and in what ways we use media in the company of others, in place of spending time with people, or even by making new contacts through shared media experiences.
- **Finances:** We spend substantial amounts of money acquiring media (attending movies; buying media such as books, music, DVDs, and ringtones; purchasing media players such as iPods and TVs; paying for cable

TV and broadband access, etc.). Personal budgets are significantly affected by our media needs.

- **Perceptions of the world:** Because we have firsthand experience with a very limited amount of reality, most of our perspective on the world is delivered by media, channeled through their filter, whether in the form of news, entertainment, or education.
- **Politics:** The election process is now a media event more than a campaign based upon in-person experiences. Our introduction to candidates and our voting preferences are significantly influenced by how those individuals are presented to us by the media. Our awareness and understanding of social and political issues have largely become dependent upon media communication and interpretation.
- **Mental and physical health:** As will be explained below, medical studies consistently indicate that exposure to audio and visual media has dramatic mental and physiological effects, such as rewiring our brains and altering our moods.
- **Morals and values:** A growing body of research is demonstrating the effects of media content on morals, such as desensitizing us to violence, changing our perceptions of the value of life, exposing us to a wider range of perspectives that influence our own views, and significantly impacting our thoughts about moral issues such as cohabitation, divorce, homosexuality, war, debt, and poverty.
- **Spirituality:** Because of exposure to a greater variety of beliefs and faith-based lifestyles provided by mass media, many people's religious and spiritual choices change. In addition, a substantial amount of spiritual knowledge is passed through media channels to end users. Also, the notion of who our spiritual leaders are has been largely shaped by media exposure and positioning.

The aspect of our media use that gets the greatest amount of attention, of course, is how much time we devote to consuming media content. We probably focus on that element for two reasons: it is easy to measure, and it reflects our obsession with it. The quantity of media exposure is important, but as we will discuss, it is not the most important factor for us to examine.

In some circles there is a reflexive tendency to dismiss all media as harmful. That's not an accurate judgment, of course. Any form of media is just a tool—a means of accomplishing a specific end. The media are useful for informing, educating, and entertaining. By fulfilling those roles, media can provide important benefits. For instance, some media tools—such as training DVDs, movies, and music—can stimulate thinking and conversation. In fact, research shows that such tools often facilitate information retention. One of the studies we conducted a few years ago showed that people are more likely to remember principles demonstrated in a brief, dramatic video clip than they are to recall the same principles described in a verbal presentation such as a sermon or classroom lecture.

Media—especially the entertainment variety—can also give people a healthy release from their daily tensions, providing a way to emotionally decompress or physically reenergize after an exhausting or intense day. Media can capture our attention and help us focus upon items of importance. And when properly used, media can facilitate language development, as well as reasoning and problem-solving skills.

In fact, most faith tribes have adopted media tools as means of advancing their communities. Think about the extensive use of media in Christian churches. A typical church these days uses big-screen video technology to show announcements, song lyrics, and message outlines; audio amplification systems for the music and speaking; digital recording of the message; online search engines to locate material used in the sermon; and various types of advertising and online messaging to encourage people to attend. A minority of churches use other forms of technology and media related to music, fund-raising, broadcasting services, online events and communications, mobile computing, and the like. Take these tools away and many churches would feel that their ministry had been irreparably harmed.

For better or worse, media have become an ingrained part of the American life.

TOO MUCH OF A GOOD THING?

I hope you can see that my intention is not to bash media. We have to objectively assess their strengths and weaknesses. In so doing, however, I have developed a hypothesis that often surprises people. It's a very simple but significant thesis: *media exposure has become America's most widespread and serious addiction.*

According to the American Psychiatric Association, an addiction is a chronic disorder in which we are unable to control our need for the substance in question and in which a combination of components are simultaneously at work. While we most often think about addictions like drug or alcohol abuse, an addiction can also "describe a recurring compulsion by an individual to engage in some specific activity, despite harmful consequences to the individual's health, mental state, or social life." (The term *media junkie* comes to mind.) Specifically, a person has an addiction if his or her use of the substance in question (in this case, media) produces clinically significant impairment or distress, in line with specific symptoms, within a twelve-month period. Those symptoms include the altering of brain function through exposure; experiencing withdrawal symptoms when use is eliminated or minimized; losing control of how much exposure he or she seeks to experience; becoming incapable of stopping exposure; abandoning or reducing his or her involvement in normal and healthy activities because of the influence of the addictive substance; and repeatedly denying that a real problem exists.

After exploring media usage patterns from our research and

that of other media research firms, it appears that a majority of Americans over the age of twelve are, indeed, addicted to media consumption. We see a steady increase in the amount of media exposure that characterizes the typical person's life. We see dogged resistance to reducing our media usage. Medical researchers have reported physiological changes resulting from our exposure to substantial quantities of media, including fewer hours of restful sleep, more aggressive behavior, obesity, shorter attention spans, and heightened levels of anxiety. We see reduced levels of participation in normal and healthy social, occupational, and recreational activities. And, of course, we have been confronted with widespread denial that there is a real problem.

If you still have doubts that we're a nation addicted to media, do a simple experiment. Ask a group of twelve-year-olds *not* to watch TV for a week. Challenge a group of juniors in high school to stay off the Internet for a week. See how willing a group of twentysomethings would be to abandon their cell phones—and, of course, text messaging—for a week. You might as well ask any of these groups of young people to stop eating for a week: it's just not going to happen!

WHAT DIFFERENCE DOES IT MAKE?

Our acceptance and reliance upon media have run the gamut, transitioning from novelty, to common practice, to habit, to obsession, to addiction. With coming advances in technology, we can expect media to be even more inescapable than they are now.

Media content is the jet fuel of our culture. We often think of media as benign transmitters of audio and visual material. But these tools have a powerful capacity to affect our lives through the messages they convey. And that's precisely why we need to reconsider how we facilitate media use in our nation.

Remember the context for this discussion: we need to restore America to strength, which will only happen if we focus on shared values drawn from the spiritual center and tacit worldviews of our seven faith tribes. To bring about that focus will require targeted leadership, family participation—and media cooperation.

Because the media paint the picture of reality that people adopt, progress can only be made if the media cooperate in this journey toward national restoration. Our objective in seeking to include the media in the restoration process is to raise the caliber of the national conversation—a dialogue that is triggered, fortified, and extended by the way the media communicate the message about who we are as a nation, our global context and common experience, and where our shared visions and goals are taking us.

The initial shift must be for media content to focus less on generating or prolonging controversy—even though it "sells"—in favor of emphasizing the consistency and stability that dominate our society, the positive progress that is regularly made within our culture across tribes and other social groups, and the encouragement to steadfastly pursue unity and peace. Such content might seem dull, but the same minds that somehow made lapses of character and judgment seem exciting and newsworthy—i.e., that bad behavior and ill intent were worth our time and focus—could certainly find creative ways to make the little victories in communities and individual lives become inspiring and informative substance for the masses.

Without a doubt, the media cherishes controversy because it attracts attention and generates revenue. But that which causes or facilitates divisiveness is detrimental to our corporate and personal well-being. And when our culture is dominated by instances of conflict and controversy at the expense of unity and understanding, the prospects for national restoration are severely diminished. Even if the controversy is over absurd distractions fabricated by paparazzi—whether a starlet was drunk onstage at an awards ceremony or a male celebrity was seen cheating on his wife—there is no socially redeeming benefit to be realized by such "reporting" or "entertainment." All that happens is the public spirit is cheapened by such worthless gossip, our lives are distracted from meaning and goodness, and our children are given errant messages about what matters and how life is to be lived.

Some social commentators have already argued that eliminating content that does not add positive value to our national character and conversation would make media content unidimensional and boring. They are missing the point. To borrow from a popular media product, the 2002 movie *Spider-Man*, "With great power comes great responsibility."[28] And there can be no debate that the media have incredible power in our culture. Now we need to hold them responsible for the power they wield.

What should the media replace divisive or degrading content with? Within responsible limitations, that's up to their creative and business savvy, but their offerings should raise our standards for life rather than plunge us to the lowest common denominator. Can we agree that the goal should be content that challenges our minds, captures our hearts, and refreshes our spirits? Can we join together in demanding content that puts us in touch with truth, beauty, hope, and meaning? Can we uniformly commit to move media away from partisan or ideological reporting of news, and beyond mindless or degrading entertainment that simply distracts us, to media that make us better people and a more respectable nation? This is not about taste; this is about providing positive value and values that advance our common national interest.

EVERYONE HAS AN OBLIGATION

If such a strategy is to see the light of day, each of us must participate in the process. You may not be a media mogul, but you can influence those who are through solidarity with your tribe.

In our free-market economy, producing and delivering media content is a business. If we, as consumers, refuse to buy the product, it will not be brought to market. That's the beauty of the free enterprise system: if there is no demand, there will cease to be a supply. Presently we get degrading and worthless content—wonderfully produced and packaged, of course—because we buy it.

Not long ago The Barna Group conducted a survey in which we discovered that nearly all parents of children under eighteen have purchased some media products for their children during the past year. When asked how comfortable they felt with the content of the media products they were providing to their children, more than nine out of ten of them said they were not comfortable with one or more of the resources they placed in their children's hands. This concern was especially acute among the parents of teenagers. The implication is that most parents feel pressured into buying products they don't like or trust and thereby tacitly endorse their children embracing the kinds of lifestyles, morals, values, heroes, language, and attitudes presented through those media.[29]

No wonder we struggle to become a united country: when the leaders of our families don't demonstrate the backbone to reject products that they themselves find distasteful or dubious, who will apply the brakes to our national demise? As consumers, we must assert our influence over those who produce resources for our consumption. We cannot be the helpless victims of garbage that is dumped upon us. We have no obligation to settle for mediocrity. It is up to us, not the media producers, to set the standards of what is acceptable and edifying content. If we exercise that influence appropriately, the standard will rise accordingly. We must stop supporting those who give us what is not good for us and that which does not satisfy our needs for quality information, education, and entertainment. Nothing creates change faster than turning off the money spigot; in this instance, that can work to the country's benefit.[30]

Where is the tribal outrage over how we are being used by the media? Why don't the leaders of our faith tribes work together to chastise media executives for misrepresenting truth? Why aren't they rising up to champion resources that promote purity, peace, self-restraint, respect, good citizenship, generosity, civility, and the other values that we share? Why do we allow ourselves to be subjected to movies, TV programs, magazine spreads, and Web sites that glamorize gruesome violence, inappropriate language and sexuality, selfish behavior, and excessive materialism? This is not about parochial morality; it is about recognizing that the moral convictions and core values of most Americans in most of our faith tribes are being ignored and challenged by an elite group of media producers who misunderstand their responsibility. But until that audience expresses its outrage, more of the same garbage will be foisted upon us.

Every nation's media content reflects its values. When you review the substance in Hollywood's movies and television programs, in our leading "gossip" magazines, or in the most popular Web sites and music tracks, does it make you proud to be an American? Knowing that this is what we export to the world and that it is how the world gets its daily exposure to what America stands for, do you feel a sense of pride and deep patriotism?

Each tribe has traditionally devoted some share of its resources to reflecting on the meaning of genuine art, beauty, love, and truth. While we may disagree on an absolute standard as to what these are, we all agree that they exist, are important, and add value to our lives. Here again is a tremendous opportunity for tribal leaders to interact with each other toward developing a shared language and vision related to our common values as presented through media. That dialogue, especially if it encompasses engagement by the tribal masses, will strengthen the bond across tribal lines and clarify what we as a nation are all about.

If you are concerned about the quality of the media that emanate from this country, the sad reality is that we have nobody but ourselves to blame for the situation. Much like the fraternity pledge who goes through a series of embarrassing and painful exercises with his soon-to-be frat brothers and, by tradition, must ask for even greater embarrassments and pain in order to successfully complete his initiation rites, our values are being dismissed and ridiculed, but we keep supporting those who defy us to stand up for what we believe.

The call for superior content must be specific, though, so let me offer some parameters to frame that discussion. We would benefit from pursuing what we might label the "high five" media production strategy. This would raise the standard for media to become:

- **High quality:** Everything should be produced with excellence, in order to honor the audience to which it is being delivered. This ranges from the production values to the storytelling, the integrity of the message to the expected value added to the consumer's life. As a people, we value wisdom and earnest effort; our media should reflect such values.

- **High principle:** The content should challenge us to be better people—intellectually, spiritually, morally, ethically, and relationally. The media we consume reflect on who we are as a people, so the media we receive should respect us as classy and discerning. For us to become people of integrity, the media we consume should model that trust through the values, morals, language, and visuals presented. Media should not attempt to manipulate people in any fashion. In fact, the values we embrace—such as being peacemakers, respectful, forgiving, civil, and generous—are tailor-made for exposition by the media.

- **High touch:** The digital media age promotes media that involve people. An involved consumer is a vulnerable consumer—so we must be careful that our inducement to participate in the exchange initiated by media produces positive and safe experiences or outcomes. Empowering people to become part of the process enhances the probability of them embracing the content. Because we value investing in upcoming generations, respecting and honoring our older adults, as well as cultivating civility and citizenship, the media that bring people together and provide them an outlet should also integrate such values into the process.

- **High tech:** Based on the personal growth facilitated by the use of the latest innovations in technology, media should capitalize upon our desire to develop by giving us content in ways that advance comprehension, recall, and application. New technologies enable us to make a more compelling case than has been previously possible; we can exploit that benefit for positive outcomes. These new alternatives can be applied to promote all of the values that we adopt.

- **High performance:** The content delivered should generate a substantial cultural return on investment by promoting the best interests of the society, based upon our shared values. The measure of success would include the cultural benefit derived. Knowing that all of our faith tribes teach the value of performing to the best of one's abilities and the benefit of demonstrating self-restraint in all matters, we have a chance to execute media messages and imagery in ways that prove our commitment to becoming a culture that embodies such values.

Such objectives do not limit our creativity or marketing potential; if anything, they enable media to be just as popular while simultaneously serving the good of society.

CHALLENGE YOURSELF

What can you do about the role and substance of media in our culture? My first exhortation is to ask that you think deeply about this matter. If the media have become addictive in our culture (as proposed earlier in this chapter), media content does not meet the standards that you would set if you were "in charge," and you have the ability to influence what the media environment looks like, then it might be helpful to begin answering a series of questions about what you will do to change media in America. At the risk of sounding like a "nagging fundamentalist" or a "narrow-minded conservative," I would urge each tribe and every individual to realistically analyze how the media we consume advance the shared values of our nation.

- What is "news"—controversial or provocative circumstances, or information about changes in the status of socially significant matters?
- Do you expect news reporting to be objective or subjective?
- Is it acceptable for "entertainment" to covertly integrate ideological messages or positions, regardless of whether they are conservative or liberal in nature?
- How well are we executing our shared values of making wise decisions, representing the truth well, and investing in young people through the media content we absorb?
- If you conclude that we need to make changes in our national media environment, how deeply are you willing to invest in helping make things right?
- How effectively are your tribal leaders empowering you to understand and address the media environment?
- How well do you understand your tribe's teachings as they relate to the effects of media on your own worldview and judgments?
- Do you generally accept media messages without critical analysis of the underlying purpose, values, and worldview of the media, or do you scrutinize such media to filter those perspectives?

THE CRIES OF "FOUL PLAY"

Listen closely and you can already hear some folks bemoaning the fact that I have suggested we curtail freedom of speech in favor of simplistic traditional family fare. I hope you realize I have done nothing of the sort.

Holding the media accountable for the content they flood the marketplace with is simply a means of getting them to act like responsible citizens. We have all kinds of shared commitments in America: standards for safe driving, healthy food, minimum educational achievement, public behavior, and so forth. Why would we not have legitimate standards for one of the most powerful influences—perhaps *the* most powerful influence—in our culture today? This is not an ideological witch hunt, nor is it about censorship. It is about holding everyone accountable to act responsibly as they exercise their freedoms.

Must we continue to play foolish games, insisting that the media have the right to degrade the audience, cheapen life, dissipate shared moral standards, and threaten the mental and spiritual health of our children?

Is there significant value to communicating to other nations of the world that the United States is so committed to the freedom of everything imaginable—moral anarchy, if you will—that we refuse to place any meaningful limitations on media content, preferring instead to protect garbage? Are we convinced that our best strategy is moral amnesia and social numbness toward an alleged right that was never provided in the first place—the right to be an accessory in the destruction of our country?

The appropriate use of media can help to heal and grow this country. It is up to our faith tribes to rise to the challenge of ensuring that media exposure elevates our nation rather than eviscerates it.

CHAPTER
TWELVE
Stepping Up the
Family's Contribution

THE family is an important element in the strength and stability of our society. Contrary to popular thought, the family experience—its practices, social expectations and roles, legal definitions and parameters, and even its self-perception—has changed dramatically over the course of American history. What has *not* shifted, though, is the value that the family has added to the nation. It has consistently served as a source of caregiving, training, relationships, bonding, and support; a means of organizing work efforts; a determinant of leisure preferences and experiences; and an arbiter of accepted rules of behavior. One of the greatest legacies of the American family has been its adaptive capacity in the context of substantial cultural change. Our families have been leaders in figuring out how to make sense of upheavals in the economic, political, and social spheres of the nation.

We are certainly living in one of those turning points of history in which the wisdom of the family unit is desperately needed to keep the country moving in the right direction.

It is no coincidence that the decline of our nation has coincided with the accelerating confluence of divorce, cohabitation, and households with two working parents. At the same time, the nation's faith tribes have also experienced heightened challenges as their families have struggled to stay together. For instance, both Christian tribes, as well as the Mormon, Jewish, and Muslim tribes, instruct their adherents to avoid divorce. Yet roughly one-third of all married adults from those tribes eventually dissolve their marriages. For many years, the United States has had one of the highest rates of divorce in the world. There is nothing on the horizon to suggest that it is likely to decline in the near future.[31]

Even though the evidence shows that the family's influence in our country is waning, it remains one of the most impactful entities in people's lives—and one of the keys to the restoration of the nation. Given its influence on the nature and direction of the culture, on the development of future generations, and on Americans' identity and community, the health and involvement of the family are crucial for our future.

INSIGHTS THROUGH RESEARCH

Recently, my company completed a multiyear examination of the lives of children. I was stunned by the results. I had entered the project well aware of the standard arguments about the importance of nurturing children: they are a gift from God, they will be our future leaders, they bring creative energy and ideas to the marketplace, and they largely define (and are defined by) pop culture (language, music, dress, attitudes, technology, adoption, entertainment, relationships, etc.).

But the research pointed out new and important insights that radically altered my thinking about, well, everything. For instance, did you know that the moral values of people are generally decided by the time they reach the age of nine? Did you know that our foundational spiritual beliefs and commitments are typically ingrained by the age of thirteen? Were you aware that relational habits and patterns are pretty much molded by the age of thirteen? The lesson was clear: how we raise children before they reach high school age determines who they become for life.[32]

We also found out that most parents say they accept the

responsibility for guiding their children's growth, but in practice they are likely to rely heavily upon the expertise of others. For instance, they count on churches or religious centers to inculcate religious beliefs and practices. They expect schools to take care of fundamental matters such as social skills, emotional guidance, behavioral training, intellectual development, and career preparation. They enroll their youngsters in after-school programs—school teams, local sports clubs, athletic leagues, and exercise programs—to foster their physical development. Other groups—Scouts, 4-H, and any of a hundred-plus youth-oriented organizations—offer additional options for personal growth. They look to the media to provide entertainment and even some educational experiences for their children.

In essence, parents have shifted from the role of primary caregivers to that of child-development managers. They have become adept at outsourcing hands-on developmental tasks while trying to stay sufficiently connected to their children to know how the process is working and to maintain a viable relationship with the youngsters.

OUTSOURCING PARENTHOOD

The outsourcing model satisfies parents for several reasons. One is that parents are constantly exhausted. In most households with children, both parents work. When they return from their paying jobs, they usually have little energy left over for their children. They do the best they can, but there's just not much in reserve. Add to their fatigue the fact that they are distracted by the numerous other responsibilities and obligations they juggle. Don't forget to throw in their natural craving for some well-deserved relaxation (TV, movies, exercise, athletics, socializing). And even though they know they are in charge of raising their children, they have never been adequately prepared for that job, which makes it even more taxing. Few parents have an adequate support system to bolster their efforts. All in all, it's a less-than-ideal scenario.

Consequently, most parents do the best they can from moment to moment, trusting that it will all work out fine in the end. They admit they are not perfect, but they believe they are doing okay. As they evaluate themselves within the parenting environment, they gain comfort from the fact that most other parents are treading the same path.

Unfortunately, the outsourcing model has satisfied one set of needs (i.e., that of tired, ill-equipped parents) but has raised a host of other issues. The tacit abdication of personal responsibility by American parents is one of the major factors that has placed this nation on the road to implosion. Consider what our research has shown the laissez-faire strategy looks like in practice:

- Core values have been inadequately passed on to young people.
- The mechanics of responsible citizenship have been marginally addressed.
- Children have received little to no education concerning what it means to be a competent follower.
- Young people have been given enormous freedom to self-govern, which has elevated the media to the role of constant babysitter and trusted friend.
- Basic skills have been ill formed: children are adept at talking but not listening, complaining but not encouraging, demanding but not thanking, starting but not finishing.
- Self-image and personal expression have trumped the importance of adding value to community.
- Expectations of quality in all aspects of personal performance have plummeted to minimal levels.

Americans have even accepted a motto to describe this approach: it takes a village to raise a child. All in all, the outsourcing model has facilitated greater selfishness among individuals and decreased bonding within families.

The magnitude of the crisis—and it is a crisis; that word is not hyperbole—is consistently ignored by leaders. In fact, political leaders have fueled the crisis by passing laws and instituting government programs that facilitate parental outsourcing.

Faith tribes have done surprisingly little to alleviate the problem. Moreover, they often exacerbate it by offering a slew of programs that remove child-raising pressure from parents: day care, after-school programs, separate youth programs, and the like. As our research in prior studies pointed out, churches and other religious centers often become codependents in this outsourcing process.

An objective assessment of the dangers facing the United States must place the collapse of the family at or near the top of the list. So what can families do to carry their share of the burden in restoring the country to greatness?

Each tribe believes that the family is important. And each tribe accepts the idea that it has a responsibility to support its families and to help them raise children to be appropriate and productive citizens. That leads to several strategies we can all agree upon—not because they are easy or appealing, but because they are necessary to produce the results that will right our sinking ship.

FAMILY, FIRST AND FOREMOST

The first step toward solving any problem is admitting that a problem exists, and that applies to the breakdown of the family. We can start by acknowledging that the family in America is weak. And then we must agree that if the family remains in its weakened and deteriorating state, American society will suffer substantial injury.

Throughout our nation's first two hundred years, the family was a reliable foundation in society. It was expected that the family would teach its children things like character qualities, social values, faith principles, citizenship, and vocational

preparedness. The major social institutions of the nation—
schools, government, churches, media, courts, and businesses—
uniformly supported families in filling that role. The result was
a nation of families who had problems but were capable of effectively handling those issues.[33]

The context in which families attempt to play their roles has
changed dramatically. What has not changed is the need for us
to invest in strengthening families to the point where they can
and will readopt their appropriate, historic role. Each tribe has a
vested interest in advancing the cause of the strong family.

Intense commitment

To begin, tribes must help adults recognize that parenting matters—so much so that they believe that *parenting is the single
most significant job they have.* During our nation's rise to and
enjoyment of greatness, the basic unit of activity was not the
individual, as it is today; it was the family.

Children rely upon their families to provide secure environments in which they receive love, respect, and acceptance, as
well as their basic needs (food, clothing, shelter, safety, and
belonging). Parenting necessarily includes teaching children
basic skills, core values, civic duties, religious beliefs and practices, and manners. Whether they like it or not, parents serve
as role models for their children since so much of what young
people learn is derived from observing and imitating those they
know and trust. Parents must pass along their heritage so that
the coming generation retains both knowledge and pride in what
it means to be American. And parents must connect their children to a larger community of people who share the same values,
a role often filled by one's tribe as well as extended family and
other connections.

Facilitating a positive family experience is a full-time occupa-
tion for both the mother and father. That does not mean they
cannot hold down external, paying occupations, but it does
imply that parents must make very careful choices and closely

monitor who is doing what with their children during those times when they are not personally in their children's presence. The typical "dump and run" strategy—leaving the kids at day care, delivering them to school, arranging for them to get to after-school programs, having a babysitter lined up when they get home, hiring tutors to help them with homework—is insufficient when it comes to producing the positive outcomes they want in their children.

To get on the right track from the start, parents must recognize that raising their children is their most important civic contribution. The tribes associated with the three largest faith systems—Christianity, Judaism, and Islam—are taught that family is of paramount importance to God. The young people we release into society some two decades after birth will influence the very nature of that society, giving parents a central role in determining the future of the world. More than voting or paying taxes, the kind of citizens parents develop will be their most significant contribution to society.

Internal leadership
To make the most of the opportunity, though, families must have strong, positive leadership from within. That means parents in every household must step up and provide visionary, focused guidance. Their efforts must be aided by a support system that provides encouragement, perspective, tools, reinforcement, and capable assistance. That's another place where one's tribe comes into play. In the midst of seeking to nurture their children in terms of values, worldview, and decision making, tribes have a chance to help shape the parents' thinking in order to pass along such perspectives to the children.

Our firm's research uncovered common approaches to parenting, including the ineffective strategy of "parenting by default," or following the path of least resistance in child rearing. Faith tribes can help parents avoid this approach by injecting direction and purpose into the parenting strategy, and by assisting parents as they seek to raise their children to be good citizens and tribal members. Because most parents are not habitual leaders—that is, people whose primary function in life is to provide leadership in most of their everyday situations—it is enormously valuable to have a faith tribe supporting parents by empowering them to provide viable situational leadership.

Unfortunately, we discovered in our research that few parents have anything beyond a vague idea of what they are trying to accomplish with their children—and even fewer have any real plan to achieve their ambiguous goals. If America is to return to greatness, parents must be clear in their own minds as to what parenting means, what they want their children to be like, and how to fulfill those responsibilities with excellence. This is an issue of establishing vision and providing the necessary leadership inside the home to convert the vision to reality.

If parents are trying to envision the type of person they are seeking to raise, one phrase that might capture the essence of that quest is this: honorable citizen. Each tribe will approach this challenge a bit differently, but this is an outcome each tribe would embrace. If we begin by creating our parenting process around the concept of producing children who add value to society by displaying breadth and depth of character, in line with the shared values of our tribes, then we are on the way to healing American society and equipping our children for productive and meaningful lives.

As you can imagine, the challenge to parents is in the commitment to shaping such character. Our research revealed that parents are much more concerned about their children's test scores and career preparation than they are about their children's character. Here again, the tribe plays a natural role by helping families identify appropriate values and character traits to pursue and to invest their parenting energies in the right outcomes.

It is in this arena that the conflict between cultural values and spiritual values arises. Many parents, regardless of tribal affiliation, have been seduced by societal mores to treasure behaviors and attitudes that foster getting ahead in material terms. While the nation's faith tribes do not march in perfect unison regarding the relative importance of material success, they do generally suggest that worldly success not be achieved at the expense of values such as integrity, honesty, serenity, respect, tolerance, civility, compassion, and consideration. For instance, it is reasonable for parents to want their children to score well on standardized tests or to place highly in educational rankings. However, parents should not demand such results if doing so leads children to cheat, become anxious, or behave inappropriately toward others.

Character development often leads to a definition of success that conflicts with the norm in our society, which is the quest for personal ascension and comfort. A tribal-influenced definition would more often than not focus upon the pursuit of truth, obedience to one's deity and faith principles, building and maintaining harmonious relationships, using one's talents to serve people and advance the good of society, and the like. Great parents, with a coach's eye for teachable moments, identify, demonstrate, refine, and reinforce desired character traits in their offspring.[34] Faith tribes have traditionally assisted parents in shaping their children's worldview, values, and character.

Parent as coach

In order to do all of this—and it is no small or simple task—parents must redesign their self-image to see themselves as parents first. This means thinking of themselves as parents, first and foremost; evaluating their lives in terms of how the parenting process is transpiring; and investing in maturing in that role.

The effective parents we interviewed taught us that success in parenting is partially about mind-set and partially about the performance of child-rearing duties. Interestingly, we found that, more often than not, the effective parents saw themselves as coaches. If you think about it, that perspective makes sense. Great coaches motivate their protégés and constantly communicate instructions that guide them to victory. Coaches must always evaluate what is going on, what works and doesn't work, and how their protégés are handling new challenges. Ultimate success requires a long-term strategy that the youngsters pursue with their coaches' guidance.

Among children's chief motivations for doing the difficult things are owning and becoming passionate about the outcomes set by their coaches. Young people adopt these outcomes once they trust that their coaches are fully committed to their success and have amply proven their capacity to navigate the challenging and unknown rapids of daily life with wisdom and skill.

Being a great parent-coach means taking charge of the process. Great coaches take full responsibility for the results of their children, while giving the credit to the children who committed themselves to full maturity. Coaches enter the process with a plan, they institute structure and regimen, and they enforce rules designed to produce specific results. Great parent-coaches are relentless in their pursuit of the designated outcomes.

In this process, parents must also pay attention to their own maturity and development. Great parents are always growing. It is a principle that enables them to have something of value to give to their children: a worthy example, useful knowledge, genuine faith, reliable advice, and more.

Tools required

Producing honorable children takes some tools. One of those is communication. We learned that great parents communicate constantly with their children. Those parents informed us that the most important factor in the communication process is listening. Raising a champion requires knowing more than the whereabouts and dietary preferences of each child. It is invaluable for parents to know what their kids are thinking and experiencing. And it is priceless for children to believe that their parents genuinely care about them and are invested in their lives.

The most important factor of all, though, may well be consistency. Grown children who have become great citizens told us that they were not always keen on the rules and limitations set by their folks, but they appreciate the foresight and backbone their parents had in consistently enforcing those parameters. According to the grown children, the structure and reliability provided by their parents was a beneficial element in the shaping of their lives.

Planning to succeed

Our research among great parents showed something else: you cannot count on raising a great child by accident. It happens, but the success rate is abysmally low and certainly not something you'd want to count on. You have to enter the process of parenting with a plan that has the hope of producing desirable outcomes.[35]

We discovered that there are laissez-faire parents (whatever happens, happens); those who engage in parenting by default (we do what society says is right or appropriate these days); trial-and-error parents (all parents are amateurs, so we keep trying things until something works; we learn as we go); and revolutionary parents (we take a goal-driven, values-based approach). Of course, the parents engaged in any one of these four approaches do not characterize their efforts in these ways, but it is essentially what occurs.

Our parenting studies indicate that a useful starting point is for parents to develop a comprehensive and coherent philosophy of parenting. This includes thinking through basic perspectives such as views on the father's role, the mother's role, educational obligations, disciplinary practices, the means to inculcate responsibility and respect, family contours, the place of faith in child and family development, individualism, meaning, and purpose. That's an awful lot to come to grips with—just as attempting to nurture a human being is an incredibly consuming challenge.

Once a view of parenting has been established, it makes sense to craft a plan that identifies particular goals, with related strategies, that will hopefully produce the desired outcomes in a child. Plans are never perfect, but they provide a sense of how to move ahead and give some ideas on how to evaluate where parents are in the developmental process. That, in turn, allows a parent to refine the plan with the ultimate vision in mind. Attempting to raise children without a grand plan, however unsophisticated it may be, is tantamount to constructing a house without a blueprint.

HOW TRIBES FIT IN

Most of our faith tribes are very clear about the significance of parenting. Facilitating awareness about the importance of child development and the shaping of its children's worldviews is one of the most significant roles the tribe provides.

Each tribe approaches the parenting challenge a bit differently. Captive and Casual Christians are instructed in the Bible to train children early so they will develop proper moral, spiritual, and lifestyle habits, and to make the family the centerpiece of one's life. The emphasis in Jewish life on the family coincides with teaching in the Torah—which Christians also embrace—to make parenting a priority. Mormons accept all of these teachings, with further emphasis on strong families added by the Book of Mormon. Muslims, at the behest of the Koran, believe that the home is to be a center of worship, teaching, life instruction, and security, all driven by adults who are focused on effectively parenting their children. Pantheists and Skeptics, while more diverse in their perspectives, also tend to take seriously their responsibilities for purposeful parenting.

Tribes can add even more value to the parenting process, beyond carrying out the functions described earlier. For instance, every tribe has traditions that assist parents in raising commendable young people. Although the children often moan about having to participate in "stupid, boring traditions" that have been handed down by family members for generations, many parents have also discovered that when those traditions are eliminated, the cry gets even more intense. When comforting and familiar elements are removed from daily life, people experience a sense of loss. Tribes can help families keep meaningful traditions alive, ranging from seasonal activities to more common expressions of personhood and faith.

Each tribe, through its organizations and relationships, can also provide opportunities for members to interact with people from different tribes. While some religious groups find the very idea of sponsoring such meetings to be threatening and potentially counterproductive, the track record of such gatherings has been quite positive. Families find their relational networks, their personal faith, and their family discussions to be enriched by the stimulation derived from an exploration of alternative faith perspectives. These gatherings are not about conversion; they are primarily beneficial for clarifying one's own beliefs and for creating positive awareness and understanding of other tribes.

Ultimately, tribes remind member families of their spiritual moorings and how their faith relates to family. Faith systems point parents back to a higher power in the search for strength, wisdom, and consistency. As parents and their children pursue maturity and seek to improve society, the basic principles of their faith will continue to expand their potential for adding value to our nation.

CHAPTER

THIRTEEN
Faith Tribes Must Pull
Their Weight

FAITH is an integral part of every person's life, even if that choice is *not* to believe in a higher power, or to believe in the existence of such an authority but to minimize the role or significance of that power in one's life. America's faith tribes represent an accumulation of people who have arrived at similar conclusions regarding spiritual matters. Given the varying points of view people have embraced, some tribes are more cohesive than others, and some have more influence in people's lives than do other tribes. But each one of the nation's faith tribes owes its existence to the fact that we live in a country that values and protects religious freedom. Americans take for granted the ability to pursue our faith of choice, with whatever degree of intensity we choose. Sometimes it takes a threat or experience of religious persecution before we vaguely recall that we consistently enjoy a tremendous privilege in being able to pursue the faith of our choice.

As with any freedom, we must be careful not to abuse such liberty. When we hear "abuse," we tend to think of egregious and obvious misappropriations of those rights. What America is presently experiencing, however, is a more subtle practice of religious abuse. We are not struggling because an evil government is forcefully wiping out the right to religious freedom. Instead, we are suffering because those who are recipients of the freedom selfishly refuse to allow people of different tribes the same experience they personally appreciate. We are in danger of losing a share of our freedom by failing to extend to others the same religious freedoms that we expect.

As noted earlier, our resident faith tribes have divergent worldviews that have helped people make sense of our complex and ever-changing reality and respond to circumstances in appropriate ways. But those same worldviews that help us handle life have also created tension and mistrust among people who hold different worldviews. With the media driving a wedge between groups possessing divergent views, we most often wind up focusing on how to defend our positions and how to protect our tribes and families from assault. Consequently, we are frequently in attack mode, even if our methods are subtle. For instance, we might gossip about the dress style, the language, or the worship customs of another tribe. We might refuse to befriend or hire people from other tribes. We might choose to move to areas where members of certain tribes don't live. We might dismiss the sacred literature of different tribes as nonsensical words of foolishness. Such covert attacks destroy the bridges necessary for our nation's faith tribes to peacefully coexist and cooperate.

By jealously guarding our individual worldviews, we lose consciousness of the twenty values that Americans share that could serve as the foundation for a national renaissance of vision and unity. Acknowledging and embracing those common values does not mean that we would all adopt the same spiritual beliefs or practices. Even if that were possible, it would not necessarily be beneficial for the nation. Acknowledging and pursuing our common values would enable us to communicate and interact more harmoniously, even as we attempt to sort out the lifestyle differences in our respective faiths.

Our faith tribes have more responsibility in this pursuit of unity than to simply sit back and teach their theological distinctions. Because each tribe has influence not only in the lives of its members but also within the culture at large, each tribe plays a critical role in establishing the motivation and the means to creating a national atmosphere of cooperation and collaboration.

With the proper leadership, our nation's tribes could move people toward a revolution of interfaith harmony that transcends the limitations inherent in pluralism or ecumenism. This would require a commitment to unity and mutual understanding ignited by the recognition that genuine freedom of religion demands each tribe coexist peacefully and amicably with other tribes.

Some people suggest that this is not the job of faith tribes, but the responsibility of political leaders and parties. I disagree. Politicians and their parties are, to some extent, the leaders who guided us into the pit in which we now find ourselves mired. They have a vested interest in supremacy and survival, neither of which is useful as we attempt to build bridges and mend broken relationships.

Politics, in its ideal form, is the art of compromise, an act of service in which people are helped to lead richer lives. In our current environment, though, politics too often becomes an exercise in selfishness, exploitation, or bullying. Until our faith tribes can transcend that environment and the values that prevail within it, we will be hampered by the ongoing bickering and mistrust that has derailed the nation. Our elected officials are not likely to instigate the rescue; it must come from our faith tribes.

Government officials rely upon laws and policies to shape society and affect people. America benefits from laws that facilitate order and freedom, but the answer to our present crisis is not more laws; the solution can come only from more understanding, commitment to shared principles and values, and a sincere desire to be an active part of a national community. Our tribes must step up to the plate and deliver what they are best at: a higher standard of character and morality to which we all relate and voluntarily surrender. Once we do so, we will have expedited the job of our governmental leaders, who can continue to provide leadership without the hostilities that paralyze the process today.

While politicians and political parties pursue and manage power, tribal leaders must guide their people toward mutual service and surrender. While elected officials and activist judges pursue their personal agendas for the future, the tribes must lead the way in identifying and adopting ways of living that promote the long-term national interest rather than short-term political or personal gain.

These advances can only be made by leaders who are more interested in national preservation than in self-preservation. They can be accomplished only by leaders who recognize that there is a greater power at work than themselves. And genuine progress is likely only if we work from a body of consensual values that promotes the common good rather than from a parcel of divisive and hostile strategies designed to divide and conquer.

At their core, faith tribes are all about experiencing and sharing authentic meaning and purpose in this life. None of our tribes believe that our ultimate purpose is political dominance. That is a coarse strategy designed to fulfill personal grandeur and comfort. As the nation's history has shown, we are a better people than that strategy suggests.

But when the traditional leaders get off track, to whom can we turn to provide the kind of sanity and focus that the nation needs during such a crisis as this? It seems most reasonable to rely upon those who lead people into reflection, goodwill, service, and community.

If that is the case, then what steps would be required of our faith tribes, recognizing that they generally stay at arm's length from each other and from any organized efforts at building a public coalition together?

SEVEN COMPONENTS OF UNITY

Based on my exploration of successful revolutions and mass movements in the recent past—that is, effective organized efforts to redefine a culture—here are seven components that would propel us closer to our goal: a truly *United* States of America. The components relate to ideology, intimacy, identity, impact, intensity, immediacy, and inefficiency.

Ideology

Each tribe provides teaching and practices that result in adherents adopting a particular worldview. As shown earlier, those worldviews are built upon a sequence of values that represent the heartbeat of the tribe. Those values become a source of tangible guidance in people's lives.

As you consider our shared values, you will notice that they tacitly confirm the benefit, if not the necessity, of connecting with other people in harmonious ways. Consequently, one element of the vision tribal leaders must cast is the importance of living as a valuable and value-adding constituent of a multitribe nation.

Each tribe possesses a unique body of spiritual truths and principles to which it is committed. But it is reasonable—and desirable—for each tribe also to embrace a body of principles and practices that display the uniqueness of the tribe that enables it to become a valuable and valued part of the nation. As described in chapter 10, each tribe must convey a compelling vision that embodies the tribe's faith standards, alongside values like being stellar citizens and neighbors, treating all people appropriately (with respect, kindness, etc.), and contributing benefits to society through productivity and reinvesting in people.

Intimacy

A tribe provides a way for people to develop meaningful connections with other like-hearted individuals. Continuing to promote solid intratribe relationships is critical toward enabling society at large to become more tightly knit. The challenge for tribes is not simply to facilitate acquaintances but to help develop an extended, faith-based family. The more deeply committed we become to the relational principles and values that drive our respective faiths, and which we share, the more likely we are to cease recognizing and reacting to the false dichotomies humans have created between each other and between groups.

The more we enable tribes to become intimate communities, the more we can use those connections as a launching pad for establishing similarly meaningful and reliable connections across tribal boundaries. Ultimately, we ought to be able to achieve true integration, regardless of our diverse religious and moral backgrounds. But our connection to a tribe can provide the moral and emotional strength, as well as the intellectual motivation, to take such a risk.

Identity

Americans juggle multiple identities. In the context of restoring America, we would be well-advised to reorder the priority of our identities and to understand our primary identity in light of the national identity.

Currently, people's dominant self-image includes that of unique individual, responsible parent or family member, productive worker, savvy consumer, citizen in good standing, reliable neighbor, and person of faith—pretty much in that order of priority. The relative ranking of those components varies from tribe to tribe, but all of those roles are deemed to be important and play a significant role in our self-view.

In fine-tuning that identity, though, we must affirm that the United States is better off due to the presence of any given tribe, but that no tribe is called or allowed to disrespect the rights or uniqueness of people from other tribes who are living within the boundaries of the shared values and laws of the country.

Alienation and insecurity are empty and painful experiences that become more likely the closer we march toward moral and spiritual anarchy. A more tenable existence—and one more in tune with tribal principles—will be experienced if we embrace the identity of being part of an extended spiritual constituency— one that is diverse in beliefs and practices, but which consists of equally valuable human beings. As we each live up to our potential to contribute meaning and value to the world, we can solidify the identity of what it truly means to be American.

Impact

While the Captives are more evangelistically inclined than most tribes, most of the tribes look favorably upon numerical growth. But research consistently shows that people are more likely to be attracted to a tribe because of the compassion and commitment of its people than because of the tribe's doctrines, ceremonies, or buildings. The message to each tribe, then, is to grab people's attention by being consistently true to the foundations of its faith, as experienced through our shared values.

Beyond growing the tribe, however, each faith clan has an opportunity to positively facilitate the maturation of society and move the United States toward becoming a globally revered and imitated society. We are far from that now: people in other nations have admired our economic growth and political freedoms, but global surveys show that few people around the world respect the moral and spiritual life of the typical American. The more frequently we can encourage and enable people in our tribes to demonstrate their faith through their lifestyles, the more respected we will be—and the greater our influence.

Intensity

American culture is incessantly distracting. The multiple diversions to which we are constantly exposed undermine our capacity to finish what we start and to perform our duties with excellence. Our engagement with so many different activities and agendas prevents us from experiencing the benefits of being intensely immersed in—and fulfilled by—the things that matter the most.

Altering this tendency is a leadership challenge: helping people to reject the distractions in order to focus on the things that will produce the greatest and most significant outcomes. Effective leaders encourage and empower people to devote themselves to the outcomes about which they are most passionate and which are most deserving of their energy because of how those results tie into the vision. It's a competitive battle: leaders from other dimensions (e.g., political, economic, and educational) will also be vying for people's attention and allegiance. Tribal leaders must understand and exploit the connection between the value of faith and the soul cravings of the individual.

Immediacy

Surprisingly, none of our dominant national leaders has sought to impress upon people the urgency of the need to restore America to true greatness. In recent political elections we've heard all about the imperative of change and the need to restore stability, but we have not received an apologetic that described the failure of the American heart and soul—only protestations about the need for new programs, different officers, restructured organizations, and more money. These arguments have completely missed the boat.

We need a rapid retooling of the national perspective on the health of the nation and the immediate need for us all to pitch in toward righting the listing ship. Tribes can effectively get the word out and build a persuasive case for the loss of a positive national ethos and the necessity of responding from a deeper, more personal place than that which is represented by the voting booth.

Inefficiency

One of the most interesting lessons of successful revolutions and movements is that they tend to be inefficient. Their messiness is a result of the high value they place on widespread and personalized participation in the cause. Rather than squelch people's enthusiasm and risk losing them altogether, great movements give people freedom to operate on their own, as long as they understand and own the central vision and values. And because every revolution, by definition, is about taking serious risks, demanding too much efficiency would only squander the creative energy of those who are willing to fight uphill battles.

Our research among religious movements over the past quarter century indicates that religious entities that worry about structure more than engagement smother their potential. Tribes can enhance the possibility of a national renaissance by getting their people excited about the prospect of being part of a living faith that infects the entire culture through their application of our shared values. Emphasizing passion over perfection will take us a long way.

A WORD TO THE CHRISTIAN-ORIENTED TRIBES

In light of all this, some thoughts are particularly pertinent to the Christ-centered tribes. If you are not part of the Captive or Casual Christian tribes, please allow me to address my spiritual kinfolk for a few pages. If you are not part of those tribes, you are welcome to sit in on this family discussion, or alternatively you should feel free to jump to the next (and final) chapter.

Christians of all flavors comprise the vast majority of the U.S. population—more than four out of five people presently align with Christianity. That reality has no connection to the quality of our faith or the way we represent Christ in this world. For whatever reasons, we have accumulated massive numbers—and whether we like it or not, that magnitude confers both a tremendous opportunity and responsibility to provide leadership. In my estimation, because leadership is about facilitating the achievement of a compelling vision of the future, we have not done a very good job of leading in recent years. It is difficult, if not impossible, to point to new horizons that have been reached through the leadership provided by followers of Christ.

As Christians, we have a vested interest in raising our level of leadership performance. After all, should the nation implode and we lose many of our freedoms, we would suffer the greatest losses. And quite frankly, given the attitudes and character qualities we possess, American Christians are not likely to thrive under persecution.

So what can we do? How should Christian leaders lead? The same way that any great leader would: by casting significant and compelling vision, motivating people to own the vision, providing practical guidance as to how to pursue the vision, mobilizing them around the tasks that will realize the vision, and amassing the resources required to complete the vision.

And just as important, how should Christians follow such leadership? By passionately immersing ourselves in following through on the visions we embrace. We cannot allow ourselves to be distracted by the sideshows the world throws in our path. If we bear in mind that the purpose of this life is to honor God by loving Him and other people, by expressing such love through obeying and worshiping Him in everything we do, and by serving other people with every ounce of strength we have, then seeing distractions for what they are becomes much easier.

Toward that end, it would be advantageous to modify our usual approach of leading, working with, and serving the needs of only those individuals who belong to our own tribe. There is a larger body of people in America who need great leaders to help them live better, more meaningful lives. That does not necessarily mean that those from other tribes who might benefit from productive and appropriate leadership emanating from the Christian tribes will therefore accept the gospel and live in strict accordance with the commands of Christ. But we have a responsibility to love and serve those people regardless.

Gaining the opportunity to lead people beyond our tribe is becoming more and more difficult for Christians. This is attributable to the increasing isolation of our tribes (and even segregation within subtribes), the increasingly negative image of Christians in the marketplace, and the growing boldness of leaders from other tribes. To add value to our society—and to honor God—we need to see leadership as an act of service, not an exercise of power, and we must function with grace and humility rather than coerciveness and pride.

It is not our duty to force everyone in America to worship the God of Israel. It is our duty to personally worship Him and to be so changed by that experience that other people marvel at the transformation happening within us.

We have not been called to treat every public gathering as a forum for evangelism. We have been called to use every public gathering as a chance to respect, love, and serve people.

Our job is not to do everything possible to avoid persecution and hardships for our faith. Jesus promises us such trials and exhorts us to accept difficult times, even unjust actions, as a way of imitating His behavior and showing our devotion to the ways of the Kingdom of God.

We ought not see leadership as a means of ensuring that Christians dominate and get the first and best of everything. Our mission includes a willingness to sacrifice what we could have so that others might live well and see the love of Christ within us. Being a leader in the midst of prosperity and opportunity does not discharge us from the obligation to ensure that the disadvantaged or those of a different point of view also receive justice.

Providing Christian leadership is more than simply opening meetings with prayers, alluding to Scripture verses amidst discussions, and maintaining a pleasant demeanor during debates. Those things are wonderful, but we are called to be so different from the world that others take notice of how we reflect, deliberate, and provide unusual wisdom. They should be struck by how respectful we are of alternative views and the compassion we consistently demonstrate to others.

The bottom line is that we have been called by God to be the Church, not simply to go to church. At the risk of employing a worn concept, we have to ask what Jesus would do in any given situation and respond in kind. That is what it means to be a Christian—to be like Christ in every respect. It is an ideal beyond our human capacity, but it is an ideal that we can approach through the empowerment and guidance of our loving God.

Granted, that strategy requires us to be so in touch with the content of the Scriptures and the voice of the living God that we can reasonably estimate how Jesus might have dealt with a situation—and then to personally exhibit the self-discipline needed to mimic His probable response. Unfortunately, whether the venue is political, educational, familial, or economic, we have emulated the Pharisees more often than we have mirrored the hearts and behavior of the Christians who assembled in Jerusalem as the initial incarnation of the Christian tribe immediately after the ascension of Christ.[36]

We often speak about wanting to be light in the darkness. America in this twenty-first century has plenty of darkness, although it masquerades as light. Are we really providing illumination? Could we do a better job of being love in the midst of ambivalence, hostility, and fear, or of delivering wisdom in the middle of a confusing and distracted culture?

What would happen to the United States if our way of leading was not based on plans and policies and did not emerge from buildings and committees, but instead was the result of the efforts of tribes whose people chose to consistently demonstrate the ways of Christ? We are so far from that possibility today that it will take some serious retooling of our lives and relationships to get there.

But we can get there! That is what great leadership does: it motivates people to turn such a seemingly unattainable vision into reality. That, in fact, is one dimension of what faith is all about: having confidence that the things we hope for but cannot see will come to pass.[37]

What would it look like for followers of Christ to be salt and light in this country? Maybe it would include the following:[38]

- We would take the initiative to develop and nurture genuine caring relationships with people of other tribes—not for the purpose of converting them (for it is only the Holy Spirit who can bring about conversion) but simply to honor God by loving and appreciating them.
- We would listen to the life stories and heartfelt concerns of others, learning more about ourselves by gaining insight into the lives of others.
- We would let our actions do our evangelizing rather

than our words, in recognition that effective evangelism is by invitation, not intrusion.

- We would take pleasure in modeling language and attitudes that demonstrate civility, compassion, respect, and honesty.
- We would seek and maximize opportunities to bless people by caring about them, showing them consistent and abundant kindness, and serving with humility and gratitude for the chance to strengthen others.
- We would resist the urge to make any kind of judgment about other people; deciding instead to improve some element of our own lives, based on the principles taught in the Bible.
- We would embrace the mind-set that we are called to collaborate, not compete, with people of different tribes, seeing them as potential teammates rather than opponents.
- We would pour ourselves into the lives of young people by utilizing moments of opportunity, in whatever ways they might emerge. This might include offering off-the-cuff encouragement, donating resources to programs and people that assist children, getting involved in schools and children's activities, praying silently for children, and so forth.
- We would demonstrate love and cohesion within the body of Christ. What an embarrassment that there are more than two hundred Christian denominations in the United States, sending the message that since we cannot agree on God's truth and principles, we have had to divide the family into splinter groups. Rather than theologically nitpicking His truth—which, frankly, is a matter of interpretation anyway—what would happen if we bonded over His truths and principles?
- We would place our faith in God and His Word, not in politics, government, and elected officials. Let's be honest: electing Christian officials has not produced gains

for the Kingdom of God because a corrupt system corrupts those who labor within it. Jesus did not come to be crowned King of the world; He came to be the King of hearts. We would do well to invest our hope in the changing of hearts rather than votes and policies.

Our leadership has been that of a people who fear the loss of power and privilege. How foolish! We have been instructed to be in this world, but not to buy into its rewards and procedures.[39] We have been granted the chance to show the world what true love looks like. We have the opportunity to be a force to be reckoned with by choosing not to be a force to be reckoned with. If we embody love in all that we do, as well as obey and worship God, no tribe, system, doctrine, or force will be able to counteract our power and influence.

The time to begin redirecting our efforts is now. The nation has a leadership vacuum waiting to be filled. That void does not require a dominant, charismatic, hyperintelligent commander; it demands consistent acts of loving leadership and service from every one of the millions of Christians in this country. It may or may not take a village to raise a child, but it certainly takes a tribe to change a nation.

We do not change a culture from the top down. A nation gets revolutionized from the bottom up. We dare not wait for the quintessential leader to dramatically appear on the scene to call us to a nationwide act of restoration.

The revolution starts with you, doing what you are capable of doing, regardless of what others are doing. Leadership is not about being or doing what is popular. It is about doing what is right, simply because it is right.

You, personally, are responsible for revolutionizing the world. You cannot do it alone, but it cannot be done without you. If you call yourself by the name of Christ—Christian, evangelical, Baptist, Catholic, fundamentalist, charismatic, disciple, whatever label or labels you adopt—then you must earn the prestige of that label through your acts of courageous and compassionate service.

Jesus told us that it is not by your words that you will be known, but by your actions—the fruit of who you are and what you believe. What you produce for the Kingdom of God is your purpose and your legacy.

What fruit will you bear in these divided and hurting times?

FOURTEEN
A Vision for Restoring America

ON THE DAY that Martin Luther King was assassinated in 1968, Senator Robert Kennedy gave an off-the-cuff campaign speech to an assembly of predominantly African American voters in Indianapolis. The aspiring presidential candidate spoke from the heart, breaking the horrific news to his audience and begging Americans during that time of crisis to see the sickness of a culture gone mad.

"What we need in the United States is not division; what we need in the United States is not hatred; what we need in the United States is not violence and lawlessness, but is love and wisdom, and compassion toward one another, and a feeling of justice toward those who still suffer within our country, whether they be white or whether they be black." He ended his emotional exhortation by entreating people to "tame the savageness of man and make gentle the life of this world."[40]

Forty years later, what progress have we made toward the goals the senator set forth that day?

We have certainly experienced a plethora of cosmetic upgrades. There is more technology and increased opportunities for every ethnic group. We live in greater comfort and have less crime. More people attend college, and we pay relatively less in taxes.

But for the most part, we remain a nation of people with a

nagging sense of dissatisfaction. We achieved our dreams, and it still isn't enough.

- We became the world's only true superpower, with unrivaled military supremacy, but discovered that being the global police force isn't all it was cracked up to be.
- We experienced unimaginable prosperity, permitting seemingly unlimited consumption, but found out that genuine joy is not derived from having more stuff, nor does it come without a price.
- We developed an unparalleled infrastructure, but we failed to maintain it and now face the consequences of aging, dilapidated systems and structures.
- We invited millions of immigrants to enjoy our freedoms, only to find that they were not always willing to embrace the responsibilities that come with citizenship.
- Our scientists and medical professionals have provided the means to a life span unmatched since the time of Methuselah, but many senior adults wonder what the big deal is about living longer.
- We have more knowledge at our fingertips than ever but seem just as stymied by the ageless questions about meaning, purpose, happiness, and fulfillment.
- We can receive a continual barrage of entertainment and in essence amuse ourselves to death but come out none the better for having escaped or been temporarily distracted from reality.

Perhaps the heart of the issue is that our most fundamental challenges are not so much process problems as people problems. Our challenges are human in nature and therefore require human solutions. Technology, information, money, buildings—they're all wonderful resources, but they are not the key to solving our problems.

HEALING THE HEART OF THE NATION

In effect, America has a potentially deadly heart condition.

Fortunately, America has a history of rising to the occasion during times of crisis. In such perilous moments, a nation's future demands that it dig deep into its soul and draw on a reservoir of moral and spiritual strength to do what is right. Otherwise, the nation will simply collapse.

A great example of how the United States has responded in past crises is World War II, when we radically overhauled the country's economy and lifestyles to facilitate a viable future. While millions of American men went off to war, millions of women went to work for the first time, many of them taking on less-than-dainty jobs in industrial settings. Manufacturing facilities were converted into munitions factories. Consumer behavior was moderated by the federal government, which limited people's ability to purchase food and other consumer goods and required ration cards to purchase everyday items such as gasoline, coffee, sugar, and meat. Even popular entertainment was redefined and muted in order to conserve resources and focus our attention on the things that mattered.

Our cherished freedom of lifestyle was hindered for several years. For instance, Americans were expected to conserve and recycle materials so that factories had the raw materials required to produce military resources. Metal, paper, and rubber, among other materials, were carefully recycled for refabrication into wartime supplies. Even people's clothing choices were restricted by government pressure to make apparel that conserved cloth and other materials. For example, manufacturers of men's clothing dropped vests, elbow patches on jackets, and cuffs on pants, all of which consumed extra fabric without any practical purpose. Women's clothing was made from a restricted range of fabrics, and the styles themselves were altered to use less fabric. Consequently, skirts became shorter and narrower, and we were introduced to the two-piece female bathing suit in the ongoing effort to save material for the war effort.

Without widespread complaint, we sacrificed our comfortable ways of life in order to protect our freedoms. We emerged from the exercise a stronger and more energized country. We simply agreed to work together to unleash our national capacity to solve problems. Toward that end we identified the enemy, followed the strategy implemented by focused and visionary leaders, persevered, and triumphed.

We can do it again, if we so choose. We face an enemy today that is different in nature but no less threatening to the survival of America. We can confront the crisis head-on, or we can surrender ground until we have lost the battle altogether. Indeed, the choice is solely ours.

Of course, preparing to fight World War II was a little different than attempting to put an amicable end to the self-imposed culture war we have been waging for the last several decades. Unfortunately, our political officials tend to fan the flames of that battle as a means to securing reelection and public support for program funding. So without political leadership to help us end those hostilities, we need to get back to the basics of what made us a strong and vibrant nation.

That means we have to acknowledge and live within the confines of our national Constitution. That document may be two-hundred-plus years old, but it is still the revered model for all democratic countries of the world. We must adhere to its parameters. The leaders we support must be individuals who see the strength in the Constitution and seek to uphold it.

We have an amazingly resilient economic system that enables us to flex with the changes in the world economy. If we play by sane rules of finance, we can restore our nation and its individuals to fiscal health for a prolonged period.

And we certainly have a group of faith tribes whose shared core values and common commitment to being people of peace and harmony can restore this country to greatness. If we return to our spiritual moorings, we can see our best qualities emerge.

Where public policy fails us, our faith can restore vitality and unity by concentrating on qualities of goodness.

ENVISION A NEW AMERICA

It has been said that you can never restore the past, and numerous failed efforts to do so seem to support that thesis. Frankly, the past had its own set of problems, so we are better off devoting our resources to optimizing the future anyway.

The future of America will depart from the past in some very significant ways. You always build the future on the sturdy foundations of the past and create new foundations where the old ones have faltered. Out of necessity, then, our future must be a blend of the old and the new.

Envision the new United States with me.

National identity

For a period in history, we were the revolutionaries, rebelling against the religious restrictions and heavy taxation of the king of England. We later transitioned into a pioneer nation, where people embraced the spirit of exploration and entrepreneurialism. In later years, our national identity shifted again as we became one of the few economic and military superpowers, influencing the lives of virtually every nation. Along with that status came record levels of consumption of everything imaginable, from entertainment to food.

But who do we want to be tomorrow?

Our shared values offer some possibilities. We have experience as a world leader, but what if we shifted our leadership emphasis to demonstrating what it means to be peacemakers, compassionate ambassadors of justice, and people who are sensitive to the basic needs of others around the world—global servants, if you will. Working in partnership with other nations of the world, we could model respect, love, generosity, and care for those who are less fortunate. Think about it: is there a nation that people around the world look to for guidance in this area? If we banded together to become the paragon of human virtue, and labored in tandem with people from around the world, what a wonderful legacy to leave to our children. Such a vision would necessitate different habits and lifestyle patterns, but we are in a situation where we will have to make such changes one way or another. It might as well be by choice rather than by default.

New ideology

As we morph into our new role, we will need to identify and embrace a new and cohesive set of ideas about what we stand for and what we believe. Certainly our Constitution gives us a solid head start toward defining this ideology. But beyond those elements, we must transcend the divisive limitations of labels and restrictive constructs such as liberal and conservative, or progressive and market driven. Those will be aspects of our revised ideology, but they cannot be a substitute for a broader base of ideals.

Our reconfigured ideology must incorporate realities such as rampant multiculturalism and religious pluralism. It must take into account the fact that the United States is no longer capable of policing the world—nor does the world want it to. It must reflect the onslaught of global commerce and the effect of communications technology. It must speak to the divergent worldviews that rule the nations of our world, as well as our response to poverty and injustice in this new global environment.

Among the questions we must answer in this new ideology is this one: who gets to set the national agenda? We are quickly transitioning from a WASP majority to a more evenly distributed population. Practically speaking, in a democracy, that reality must influence the way in which we make decisions and arrive at a consensus. Indeed, every choice has consequences, and the nation's determination to welcome millions of immigrants in recent years has brought about some outcomes for which we were not prepared in terms of cultural assimilation. Whatever new ideology we craft must anticipate such consequences as the country reengineers itself.

New community

Historically, the United States permitted individualism within the framework of the rule of law, relying on our key social institutions (family, churches, schools, and others) to handle the acculturation of young people and immigrants. The expectation was that people would understand and adopt the dominant values and principles of the larger community and become active participants in their local communities.

This process has become much tougher in recent years. Our institutions are struggling for survival and redefinition, which has caused them to focus on matters other than their traditional endeavors. As a result, our national expectation of conformity to the norms of society has been replaced by people's preference for individual choice.

As we move into our next era as a nation, however, we must once again recognize that individualism feels good but detracts from the strength of society. While there is no value in producing a nation of clones, and we would diminish our country's capacity by insisting on wholesale conformity, developing a more advanced sense of community will enable us to restore the United States to greatness without impinging on our core freedoms. In other words, we may still experience the privilege of being free individuals, but we must do so within the context of being committed to the concepts of nation and community. That commitment will sometimes restrict the outer edges of personal expression and choices, but it is one of the sacrifices we all make for the pleasure of living in a great country.

New leadership

Turning a new leaf will not happen without competent leaders who gain widespread ownership of the vision for a new nation. By using their skills and insights, Americans can both strengthen this larger vision and maximize their personal potential.

Our future leaders will have to discover how to evaluate progress and success beyond the traditional economic and political measures. If our goal is to develop a nation in which people are able to experience personal growth and transformation in the company of a caring and supportive community, then our leaders must redefine the ways in which we assess how we are doing and what future strategies will push us closer to achieving the things that matter most.

RETAINING THE OLD

There will be some classic elements of the American experience we will certainly want to retain. Naturally, the excitement of building something new or the joy of being able to jettison that which did not seem to work raises questions about why we would retain anything from the past. There are two significant reasons. First, the practical reality is that it is impossible for a country to completely disassociate from its history. Life is a continuum, so we necessarily develop our future in light of our past, for better or worse. Second, if we were able to totally cut our ties with the past, all that we'd have left would be a focus on self, leaving us unidimensional and untethered from the victories and lessons of history, and ill-equipped to create a better future.

Some of the desirable elements we should retain include the shared values we have identified, the natural and normal responsibilities that coincide with freedom and our values, and the personal disciplines that allow Americans to be good citizens.

These proven components of greatness can be blended into the newer elements described above. The result should be a dynamic combination that produces a society that is current in its form, efficient in the delivery of opportunities and rewards, and effective in its ability to master the ways of the new world without compromising the core values and standards embraced by the country.

THE ROLE OF FAITH TRIBES

To facilitate the success of the United States in this new era, faith tribes must play a substantial role in moving people along. Our country's past success was built on the "hardware" side of the equation—that is, building the infrastructure, empowering commercial enterprise to flourish, bolstering our military presence, and ensuring a quality education for everyone. These were outcomes from processes and systems that allowed America to thrive. But without a population that has character and vision for humanity and humane behavior, even the most flawless systems and procedures merely generate goods and services. Those facets are good and necessary, but they are not enough.

Tribes can help us build the "software" side of the equation and expand the depth of America. They can assist their members in developing the heart required for the future—a heart that deploys our values to good effect.

Faith tribes will model the development of genuine relationships by establishing open dialogue with each other. Such conversation will benefit the country by establishing what we have in common, by reducing our worries and fears about each other, and by enabling us to pursue truth in tandem and to learn important lessons from each other. These interactions will naturally soften our language and images to create more respectful and palatable relationships.

Every country depends upon the narrative it projects for itself. The American narrative is outdated; now is an opportune moment to construct a new story about our views, values, and vision. As tribes interact, they will have the chance to compose a new generation of narratives to tell the story about who we are. These narratives can serve as an internal rallying point, as well as a means to help outsiders grasp what it means to be American and how to viably connect with the United States.

A hidden benefit of these dialogues will be to break down the false barriers to a deeper connection. People from other tribes, with their divergent worldviews and spiritual practices, can seem threatening. The more we are able to build bridges of respect and trust, the greater will be our nation's enthusiasm for working together and raising the standards of performance. Past cross-tribal experiences have also shown the potential for discovering or rediscovering aspects of one's own faith through the conversations that bring clarity to our own beliefs and experiences.

THE POWER OF FAITH

For many years, intellectuals have been telling us that faith would soon fade away as people awoke to the frivolous nature of belief in a higher power. Dismissing Christianity, Judaism, Islam, and other religions as mythology because the critical foundations of those faiths could not be proven, the intelligentsia is still waiting for Americans to abandon their faith and its principles. Based on what we find in our national studies, the highbrows have a long wait before we are likely to see faith fall by the wayside.

Americans may disagree on core spiritual beliefs, but they are not about to reject the entire dimension because of conflict or ambiguities. They will not surrender their faith because they cannot: too many times it has proven to be too real to them, and their faith continues to be an unassailable source of reasonable hope in an otherwise unreasonably hopeless world.

After all, what are the alternatives? Rely upon politicians and bureaucrats, and the systems they offer? Trust the business world and the marketplace to solve life's deepest issues? Simply live for pleasure and allow the entertainment industry to rule our lives? Believe the theories and spin that the educational system offers as "truth"—until new discoveries or revelations shatter those pronouncements?

No, the American people know a smart move when they see it. The power of faith is something they are not about to forsake. It is in their best interest. More important, it is in the public's best interest.

Admittedly, diverse faiths (even as distinguished from religion) can create a culture of separation in which fragmentation and compartmentalization become the norm. But ironically, when the members of a faith tribe depend on their religious beliefs and spiritual connections to provide positive value, faith actually becomes the path to overcoming such alienation and isolation. At its best, faith can bolster people by providing meaning, hope, health, and a cohesive narrative to make sense of one's life and give it direction.

The future of America is at stake. That future can best be advanced by the efforts of our faith tribes. Play your role in the process to help restore vitality to America. Your life, and that of millions of other people, will be the better for it.

ONE

A Summary of Common Worldviews Held by Americans

IF YOU'VE done much reading on the dominant worldviews, you are aware that there are a half dozen or so that encompass most people's perspectives. For the sake of clarity, let me summarize the major worldviews held by Americans today.

Keep in mind that each of the worldviews presented below is described in its pure or ideal form. Nobody has a worldview that exactly conforms to the ideal. Every person we have ever interviewed on these matters has held a hybrid worldview—that is, a perspective that combines pieces of two or more worldviews into something that makes sense to that person. It is the same way that millions of Christians claim to accept the Bible as literal truth but personally possess beliefs that are clearly at odds with what Scripture says. And if we accept the notion that the clearest window to your worldview is not what you say you believe but what you actually do, then the gap grows even wider.

NATURALISM OR SECULAR HUMANISM

This perspective is based on the notion that God does not exist; all that exists is what we can see, touch, feel, taste, and hear. Human beings are the highest form of life, and everything possible will be done to enable them to lead good and satisfying lives within the boundaries of the universe. Rather than sacred texts, the source of objective truth is the scientific method, where logic, reason, and proof reign. In this view, matter and the universe have always existed and continue to operate as a unified machine. History and human life have no purpose beyond comfort, dignity, and community. There are no absolute moral truths, and there is no life after death or eternal judgment. This life is all there is, and every effort will be made to understand it and to optimize it through reason, ethical behavior and standards, and justice.

NIHILISM

This might be understood as the "anti-world worldview" because it contends that everything is random and imagined: nothing is real. There is no self-consciousness, no real knowledge, no meaning, and no intrinsic value to life. Nihilists contend that life is complete emptiness and utterly pointless: we live, we suffer, and then we die. In the course of life, because there is no meaning or value, everything is permissible, but nothing is fulfilling. To live is to experience complete despair, without ever attaining significance, dignity, or worth. If God exists, which nihilists doubt, then God has become irrelevant because He is not recognized or accepted as the fountainhead of morality or truth. Life has earned our apathy and complete disregard for the spirit.

EXISTENTIALISM

In this view, life is absurd: it is a tale of suffering and death. Life has no objective meaning, so our days on earth are spent attempting to create meaning. We are entirely free to do so, and we are completely responsible for what we create as we fulfill our life's purpose—escape from boredom. This entire charade is conducted within a context of chaos and meaninglessness. There is no absolute moral truth; all we have are personal preferences to guide us. The futility of life is ultimately what stirs the greatest passion within us. Authenticity is highly valued, but it is achieved almost exclusively by recognizing the absurdity and randomness of life. There is no God according to this outlook, because a genuine deity would never create such a meaningless, hopeless, painful, and chaotic world. We pass our time alienated from all things that we imagine to be valuable and good: relationships, deity, and purpose.

POSTMODERNISM

This is the most commonly held worldview in the United States today. It maintains that there is no "metanarrative" or grand story that explains life and reality or gives it purpose. Each person has his or her own experience, which cannot be denied or rejected by anyone else; it is simply that person's understanding of reality and truth. Each person makes decisions about how to live based on feelings and experience—and because there are no absolute moral truths that can be known by humanity, nobody has the right to dismiss any of those decisions as wrong or inappropriate. Similarly, it is inappropriate to try to impose a moral point of view on people; morality is a private matter, and if a choice is deemed right by someone, it is therefore right for that person and others must be tolerant of that choice.

To the postmodernist, life is a random series of subjective experiences, and a person's ultimate purposes are comfortable survival and personal expression. The things that matter most in life are having experiences and relationships. Connection to groups of people is particularly important to effectively shape one's views and experiences. One may believe in the existence of God but cannot compel anyone else to do so; it's a personal choice, just like anything else.

EASTERN MYSTICISM

This worldview, like some of the others, comes in a variety of forms: Zen Buddhism, Transcendental Meditation, and Hinduism are some of the best known. This perspective is difficult for most Westerners to grasp because it operates on different philosophical rules and assumptions. In essence, everyone is god or is connected to a universal power, but divinity is an abstract, impersonal concept (unlike a Christian, Jewish, or Muslim notion of a personal God). Deity, in this worldview, is not a spiritual being who is holy, powerful, loving, and creative but a condition of the universe. History has little bearing on the present or future, reality is illusory, logic is circular, and time is cyclical, as best evidenced by the belief in reincarnation.

This group believes there is no absolute moral truth or ultimate judgment, although our future lives are likely to be affected by how we live our current lives. All matter has always existed and always will. We live within a hierarchy of material and immaterial things, with the objective of striving to attain harmony with all things. The ultimate goal of life is to achieve unity with the universe.

CHRISTIAN THEISM

This view is based on the notion that an eternal, omnipotent, omniscient, holy God created the universe and all known matter, including human beings. He is a God of order and predictability. He made earth for us to inhabit and desires a personal relationship with us, although He is Spirit and we are flesh. He has demonstrated the ultimate love for humanity by sending Himself, in the embodiment of Jesus Christ, as a relational bridge, overcoming humanity's imperfections and impure desires—i.e., sin, which is any offense against God and His law. He provides us with His expectations in the written form of the Bible, which defines immutable principles for appropriate living. The Bible provides the absolute moral truths upon which His ultimate judgment will be based, although escaping eternal punishment can be achieved solely through the grace extended by Christ. The purpose of life on earth is to worship, love, obey, and serve God. After a person dies, his or her eternity will be spent in heaven or hell, based on that person's response to God's offer of grace through Christ.

APPENDIX

TWO

Selected Survey Data
Comparisons across Tribes

THE DATA included in the following pages is drawn from the 567 variables included in this research project. (For more details on how the research was conducted, consult appendix 4.)

Variable (in percents)	Captives	Casuals	Jews	Mormons	Pantheists	Muslims	Skeptics
Stressed out	20	34	30	43	30	30	31
Deeply spiritual	94	59	38	87	54	62	24
In serious debt	12	14	15	5	11	16	13
Transformed by faith	93	52	27	85	28	71	11
Top life priority:							
Faith	41	10	2	5	5	21	2
Family	40	54	56	77	43	54	52
Success/lifestyle	6	11	13	8	21	4	17
Health	5	10	15	6	3	*	9
Activities in past 7 days:							
Discussed morality	77	56	62	71	55	79	54
Turned off immoral TV	60	39	35	53	31	55	30
Recycled materials	65	63	79	57	82	77	70
Viewed pornography	11	22	27	8	25	8	31
Got drunk	2	12	13	7	27	*	21

* denotes less than one percent

Variable (in percents)	Captives	Casuals	Jews	Mormons	Pantheists	Muslims	Skeptics
Discussed faith	72	44	55	71	45	56	38
Intimate sexual encounter/physical relationship with someone to whom you are not married	4	11	14	3	13	0	21
Read for pleasure	71	57	72	71	65	63	55
Gambled/placed a bet	15	29	26	9	24	10	25
Presidential voting:							
2004—Bush	65	41	21	78	7	7	24
2004—Kerry	23	44	67	15	74	71	57
2000—Bush	69	45	14	67	25	NA	24
2000—Gore	20	37	71	16	45	NA	49
Have made a personal commitment to Christ	100	74	15	92	17	29	22
Believe absolute moral truth exists	67	35	23	53	26	28	18
Strongly agree: Bible is totally accurate in all principles it teaches	86	42	17	30	12	18	11
Strongly agree: your faith is very important in your life today	100	71	49	89	53	78	25

Variable (in percents)	Captives	Casuals	Jews	Mormons	Pantheists	Muslims	Skeptics
Strongly agree: Bible, Koran, Book of Mormon all teach the same principles	11	23	23	53	38	50	26
God is the all-knowing, all-powerful Creator of the universe who still rules it today	100	72	36	84	22	74	23
Primary purpose of life is to love God with all your heart, mind, strength, and soul	96	66	24	84	28	64	15
The Bible is the Word of God and can be interpreted literally	43	25	11	13	11	*	5
Religious activity in the past 7 days:							
Went to religious service	100	41	21	73	16	24	5
Prayed to God	100	89	65	95	53	86	36
Read the Bible	100	34	22	67	11	32	12
Concerned about moral condition of the United States	97	85	71	93	71	67	60
Consider self to be full-time servant of God	85	58	32	71	30	56	11

Variable (in percents)	Captives	Casuals	Jews	Mormons	Pantheists	Muslims	Skeptics
Currently married	67	53	53	73	51	51	44
Caucasian	69	65	85	86	28	19	66
Household income more than $75,000	18	18	31	19	29	27	22
Have children under age 18 in household	37	35	31	43	34	47	32
College graduate (4 year)	38	31	60	35	57	39	40
Age 18–29	11	18	19	19	33	33	30
Homosexual/lesbian	1	3	2	2	4	NA	5
Median annual giving to places of worship	$1,643	$151	$78	$1,680	$36	$461	$**
Sample size	5,036	20,562	612	399	427	135	3,262

Total sample size: 30,433

*denotes less than one percent; ** denotes less than one dollar*

215

America's Shared Values

EACH tribe has its own sacred literature or authoritative works that discuss the core values of that faith community. Shown below are some of the indicators of the twenty values that America's faith tribes share.

1. Represent the truth well
2. Develop inner peace and purity
3. Seek peace with others
4. Demonstrate wisdom
5. Be forgiving
6. Practice self-restraint
7. Get yourself together before criticizing
8. Invest in young people
9. Respect life
10. Treat others how you want to be treated
11. Be a good citizen
12. Justify people's respect
13. Avoid harmful behavior
14. Honor the elderly
15. Be generous
16. Do not judge or condemn others
17. Be mutually respectful of human rights
18. Cultivate civility
19. Belong to a caring community
20. Facilitate basic skills

APPENDIX
FOUR
Description of the
Research Methods

THE primary source of research data for this book is a series of nationwide surveys conducted by The Barna Group of Ventura, California, between 2000 and 2008. In total, 30,433 surveys were conducted and used in compiling the data for this book. Each of those surveys was based upon representative samples of 1,000 or more adults, most of which were conducted via telephone. (There were a handful of surveys that incorporated some online interviews.) The sample of people interviewed in each study was chosen using random selection methods for all households with telephones within the forty-eight continental states. The response rates for those surveys ranged from 55 percent to 82 percent and averaged 61 percent.

In each survey conducted, a standard process was followed. Each household involved in the sample was randomly chosen to fit within a state-by-state quota designed to approximate the distribution of the adult population by state. The adult in the household was selected using a process of rotation on the basis of gender and age. If no qualified respondent answered the telephone, the household was called back multiple times (up to a dozen attempts) on different days of the week and at different times of the day, in an attempt to have a truly representative sample. The initial contact attempts were made on weeknights (after 5 p.m.) and on weekends. A percentage of the completed calls were verified by field supervisors to ensure valid completions.

Each survey included standard batteries of demographic and theolographic questions. (We have defined theolographics as matters pertaining to what people believe, how they practice their faith, the role of faith in their lives, how spirituality and faith become integrated into their daily experiences, and so forth.)

In total, the database included 31,198 interviews with adults eighteen years of age or older. However, 765 of those interviews were deleted from the base due to missing data that prevented us from being able to categorize those individuals regarding their faith tribe. Once we established the tribe and assigned people to each of the seven tribes, we then analyzed the data associated with each tribe in relation to 576 distinct measurement variables. These indicators covered areas such as self-image, attitudes and perspectives, lifestyle activities and preferences, goals, moral views and behaviors, worldview perspectives, religious beliefs, religious behavior, media and technology ownership and use, family experiences and perspectives, parenting views and behavior, and demographics.

While the entire database is quite large by conventional survey research standards, much of the analysis contained in these pages is based upon comparisons across faith tribes. Consequently, the profiles of each tribe must be understood in light of the number of interviews completed with members of each tribe. The degree of sampling error—that is, the amount of error contained in the statistics based on using a representative sample of that population group, rather than a census of all of the group's members—varies considerably. We can be quite confident that the information regarding the entire populations of Captives, Casuals, and Skeptics included in this study is reliable to a very high degree of accuracy. The samples of Jews, Mormons, and Pantheists are smaller, so there is a higher degree of sampling error associated with those groups (ranging between 4 to 5 percentage points from the data generated in the surveys). The most problematic group, in terms of sampling error, is the Muslim tribe, which has a sampling error of plus or minus 9 percentage points, when analyzed in its entirety.

In total, the study involved 5,036 Captive Christians (16 percent of the total); 20,562 Casual Christians (68 percent of the total); 612 Jews (2 percent of the total); 399 Mormons (1.3 percent of the total); 427 Pantheists (1.4 percent of the total); 135 Muslims (0.4 percent of the total); and 3,262 Skeptics (11 percent of the total).

Because many of the questions examined in this research were not asked in every survey, we do not have a sample size of the entire faith segment to work with, which thus raises the estimated sampling error and makes analysis more tenuous. In cases where the case size dropped below fifty people for a given tribe, that variable was not included in this analysis so as to preclude unwarranted statistical conclusions. You will note that this has a dramatic effect on our analysis of the Muslim tribe, greatly limiting the breadth of the profile we could provide for that tribe. In such cases, we searched for external research that might be useful as a supplement to our studies, being careful to look for similar definitions of the tribes across studies before incorporating any external data into this analysis.

ENDNOTES

1. For a more extensive discussion of such historical patterns, see Jaques Barzun, *From Dawn to Decadence* (New York: HarperCollins Publishers, 2000); Jim Nelson Black, *When Nations Die* (Carol Stream, IL: Tyndale House Publishers, 1994); Paul Kennedy, *The Rise and Fall of Great Powers* (New York: Vintage Books, 1987); and Arnold Toynbee, *Change and Habit* (Oxford: Oneworld Publications, 1992).

2. The limited impact of the organized church on people's lives is discussed in various publications based on national research by The Barna Group. Among the relevant sources are: George Barna, *Revolution* (Carol Stream, IL: Tyndale House, 2005); George Barna, *State of the Church 2006* (Ventura, CA: The Barna Group, 2006); David Kinnaman, *unChristian* (Grand Rapids, MI: Baker Books, 2007); George Barna, "New Marriage and Divorce Statistics Released," *The Barna Update* (31 March 2008), http://www.barna.org/FlexPage.aspx?Page=BarnaUpdate&BarnaUpdateID=295; George Barna, "Survey Reveals the Life Christians Desire," *The Barna Update* (21 July 2008), http://www.barna.org/FlexPage.aspx?Page=Barna Update&BarnaUpdateID=303; George Barna, "Christian Parents Are Not Comfortable with Media but Buy Them for Their Kids Anyway," *The Barna Update* (19 November 2007), http://www.barna.org/FlexPage.asp x?Page=BarnaUpdate&BarnaUpdateID=284; and other articles accessible from www.barna.org.

3. For additional information about the immigrant assimilation process occurring in the United States these days, see Mollyann Brodie and others, *2002 National Survey of Latinos* (Menlo Park, CA: Henry J. Kaiser Family Foundation and Washington, D.C.: Pew Hispanic Center, 2002), http://pewhispanic.org/files/reports/15.pdf; Roberto Suro and Gabriel Escobar, *2006 National Survey of Latinos* (Washington, D.C.: Pew Hispanic Center, 2006); Edwin Meese and Matthew Spalding, "The Principles of Immigration" (Washington, D.C.: The Heritage Foundation,19 October 2004), http://www.heritage.org/Research/GovernmentReform/bg1807 .cfm; Matthew Spalding, "Making Citizens: The Case for Patriotic Assimilation" (Washington, D.C.: The Heritage Foundation, 16 March 2006), http://www.heritage.org/Research/PoliticalPhilosophy/fp3.cfm; Matthew Spalding, "Strengthen Citizenship in INS Reform" (Washington, D.C.: The Heritage Foundation, 8 April 2002), http://www.heritage.org/ Research/GovernmentReform/EM809.cfm; and the U.S. Department of Education, Institute of Education Sciences, National Center for Education Statistics, *National Assessment of Adult Literacy* (Washington, D.C.: 15 December 2005).

4. In one of the paradoxes of our age, it seems that there is often an inverse correlation between information availability and how well-informed a person becomes. With the proliferation of digital technologies, more information than ever before has become accessible to Americans. Yet, in order to handle this avalanche of information, Americans have developed a filter that screens out information in which they have little initial interest or which appears to present a perspective (e.g., ideological, spiritual, historical) with which they are not comfortable. The result is that people become more isolated in a universe of people and narratives that reflect their existing worldview and predispositions, without gaining exposure to a balance of information that might threaten or otherwise alter their perceptions.

5. Matthew 5:37, NIV

6. See Don Eberly, *Restoring the Good Society* (Grand Rapids, MI: Baker Books, 1994); Charles Colson, *The Good Life* (Carol Stream, IL: Tyndale House, 2005); Don Eberly, ed., *Building A Healthy Culture* (Grand Rapids, MI: Eerdmans Publishing, 2001).

7. See publications such as Andrew Kohut and Bruce Stokes, *America against the World* (New York: Henry Holt & Company, 2007); reports from the Gallup World Poll, parts of which can be accessed at http://www.gallup.com/consulting/worldpoll/111220/Free-Limited-Version-Gallup-WorldView.aspx; and Sonni Efron, "America's Got an Image Problem," *Los Angeles Times*, July 31, 2002, A9, which describes global research conducted by the Council on Foreign Affairs.

8. Among those fundamental beliefs were the following: that the God of Israel is the one, true God; there is absolute moral truth; the purpose of life is to honor God; the family unit is ordained by God as a means to maturation and the experience of unconditional love; government is ordained by God to facilitate an orderly and meaningful life; every human being has dignity and deserves respect; every person is obliged to do what is just and right; and the community has a right to enforce appropriate moral standards. These and other beliefs are evident in the writings of the Founding Fathers and the leading religious figures of the day.

9. The information presented in chapters 2 through 8 is based on thousands of opinions culled from the people being profiled. Clearly, not every member of any tribe thinks or behaves in exactly the same way. The data we have gathered provides an overview of each faith group as a whole. (For more information about the procedures used, read appendix 4, which describes our research methodology.)

10. People's behavior is based on what they believe to be right, true, and appropriate, which is derived from their worldview. Everyone has a worldview, although relatively few people have a biblical worldview.

People's worldview is not based upon what religious group they affiliate with or how often they attend religious services and events. It is a mental, emotional, and spiritual construct that serves as a filter for their interaction with the world. People who have a biblical worldview respond on the basis of their understanding and application of biblical principles. Such individuals rely upon the teachings of the Bible as the foundation of their thinking and resulting action. For more information about the development of a worldview, see George Barna, *Think Like Jesus* (Brentwood, TN: Integrity Publishers, 2003); Charles Colson and Nancy Pearcey, *How Now Shall We Live?* (Carol Stream, IL: Tyndale House, 1999); James Sire, *The Universe Next Door* (Downers Grove, IL: InterVarsity Press, 1997); Arthur Holmes, *Contours of a World View* (Grand Rapids, MI: Eerdmans, 1983); David Naugle, *Worldview* (Grand Rapids, MI: Eerdmans, 2002); and W. Andrew Hoffecker, ed., *Revolutions in Worldview* (Phillipsburg, NJ: P&R Publishing, 2007).

11. In national research studies conducted by The Barna Group, people are categorized as "evangelicals" by meeting specific theological criteria. The criteria include people who say they have made a personal commitment to Jesus Christ that is still important in their life today; believe that after they die they will go to heaven because they had confessed their sins and had accepted Jesus Christ as their Savior; say their faith is very important in their life today; believe they have a personal responsibility to share their religious beliefs about Christ with non-Christians; believe that Satan exists; believe that eternal salvation is possible only through grace, not works; believe that Jesus Christ lived a sinless life on earth; assert that the Bible is accurate in all that it teaches; and describe God as the all-knowing, all-powerful, perfect deity who created the universe and still rules it today. Being classified as an evangelical is not dependent upon church attendance or the denominational affiliation of the church attended. Respondents are *not* asked whether or not they describe themselves as evangelical.

12. Paul used this self-description in opening his letters to the Romans (Romans 1:1) and to Titus (Titus 1:1). This identity must have been a common perspective among the early followers of Christ, though, because it was also used in the opening of the letters written by James (James 1:1), Peter (2 Peter 1:1), and Jude (Jude 1:1).

13. Examples of moral truths they teach that conflict with common media messages are that lying, cheating, and stealing are always wrong; sexual intercourse is to be reserved for one's spouse; gossip is inappropriate; and success is about obedience to God, not mastery of the world.

14. Arthur Blecher, *The New American Judaism* (New York: Palgrave MacMillan, 2007). Chapters 1 and 2 provide as good a summary as I have seen of the recent experience of the Jewish people.

15. Ibid., 205.
16. *National Jewish Population Survey 2000–01* (New York: United Jewish Communities, 2003), 7, http://www.ujc.org/njps.
17. Part of the reason Jews are comparatively less interested in "having a high-paying job" is that they are more interested in owning the company that provides such jobs to others. There is a strong entrepreneurial spirit within the Jewish community.
18. *National Jewish Population Survey*, 18–19.
19. Ibid., 7.
20. *Muslim Americans* (Washington, D.C.: Pew Research Center, 2007), http://pewresearch.org/assets/pdf/muslim-americans.pdf. Much of the data in this paragraph is drawn from this excellent study of the American Muslim population. This study was based on interviews with a random sample of 1,050 Muslim adults living in the United States.
21. Ibid., 2, 80.
22. Ibid., 7, 41, and 44–45.
23. Ibid., 23–37.
24. For an interesting discussion of this distinction, provided by someone who was formerly a believer, then an atheist, and now a leading agnostic, see Michael Shermer, *How We Believe* (New York: W. H. Freeman and Company, 1998), 7–10.
25. Ibid., 75–78, 243–55.
26. The fifteen core competencies leaders must supply in order to lead effectively are vision, motivation, mobilization, direction, leader training, evaluation, developing a healthy organizational culture, delegation, systems development, team building, multitasking, resource management, environmental assessment, developing followers, and resource development. The research is clear that no leader is highly developed in all of these qualities, which is why team-based leadership is always the most effective strategy for producing significant, vision-driven results. For more information on how team-based leadership works, our research on the topic is described in George Barna, *The Power of Team Leadership* (Colorado Springs, CO: WaterBrook Press, 2001).
27. 1 Corinthians 6:12
28. Stan Lee, Steve Ditko, and David Koepp, *Spider-Man* (Columbia Pictures, 2002).
29. This study was conducted by The Barna Group among a nationally representative sample of 601 Christian parents (Captives and Casuals) in November 2006.
30. Another option is to affect media by encouraging media producers to revise their ideas of acceptable content through the provision of incentives and rewards. Such encouragement could come in the form of standards related to public recognition, marketplace advantages, professional

or financial awards, or even license renewals (radio and TV stations generally have to meet government criteria to have their license to broadcast approved). At the same time, withholding such rewards from those media who do not demonstrate responsible behavior will reap benefits. This strategy, by the way, should include the strict enforcement of existing laws and policies regarding media content. This is not suggested in order to create a morality police or Department of Media Taste but as a means of aligning all that we do to protect the freedoms we enjoy from senseless and unnecessary erosion.

31. U.S. divorces rates are high, but international comparisons can be a bit misleading. Some of the more "progressive" countries have lower divorce rates, in part, because many of their citizens live together without a marriage ceremony or legal documentation. The pattern, however, does indicate that divorce has more than doubled in the United States in the past century. It appears to go through periods of increase followed by stabilization at the new level, rather than a gradual and continual increase.

32. The research produced two books describing the findings. One is George Barna, *Revolutionary Parenting* (Carol Stream, IL: Tyndale, 2007). This contains our analysis of how parents were able to raise children who became committed Christians. The other book is George Barna, *Transforming Children into Spiritual Champions* (Ventura, CA: Regal Books, 2004). This book is primarily about how parents and Christian churches interact and what churches can do to foster better results.

33. Stephanie Coontz, *The Way We Never Were* (New York: Basic Books, 1992); Steven Mintz and Susan Kellogg, *Domestic Revolutions* (New York: Free Press,1989); Anya Jabour, *Major Problems in the History of American Families and Children* (Belmont, CA: Wadsworth Publishing, 2004).

34. The Scriptures of the Christian, Jewish, and Muslim faiths identify several dozen desirable character traits that the tribes promote. Our research among effective parents, as described in *Revolutionary Parenting*, found that those parents tended to pour themselves into developing an average of about twenty of those attributes within their children. The characteristics most commonly pursued were compassion, love, joy, kindness, consistency, loyalty, self-control, stability, discipline, maturity, justice, sincerity, encouragement, mercy, gentleness, patience, honesty, perseverance, humility, reliability, and trustworthiness.

35. The lessons drawn from families in which the children became stellar examples of the beliefs and behavior promoted by the tribe (in this case, Captive Christians) are contained in *Revolutionary Parenting*.

36. This gathering is described in Acts 2.

37. Hebrews 11:1

38. This is not intended to be an exhaustive list. Hopefully, you will catch the spirit and flavor of these decisions and will be able to add more ideas that you can personally pursue.
39. John 17:14-18
40. "Robert Kennedy: Delivering News of King's Death," *Morning Edition*, National Public Radio, April 4, 2008.

BIBLIOGRAPHY

Ali, Abdullah Yusuf, trans. *The Qur'an*. Elmhurst, NY: Tahrike Tarsile Qur'an, 2003.

Anderson, Kerby. *A Biblical Point of View on Islam*. Eugene, OR: Harvest House, 2007.

Ankerberg, John, and Dillon Burroughs. *What's the Big Deal about Other Religions?* Eugene, OR: Harvest House, 2008.

Barna, George. *Revolution*. Carol Stream, IL: Tyndale House Publishers, 2006.

———. *Revolutionary Parenting*. Carol Stream, IL: Tyndale House Publishers, 2007.

———. *Think Like Jesus*. Brentwood, TN: Integrity Publishers, 2003.

———. *Transforming Children into Spiritual Champions*. Ventura, CA: Regal Books, 2003.

Barzun, Jacques. *From Dawn to Decadence*. New York: HarperCollins, 2000.

Bellah, Robert, Richard Madsen, William M. Sullivan, Ann Swidler, and Steven M. Tipton. *Habits of the Heart*. Berkeley, CA: University of California Press, 1985.

———. *Individualism and Commitment in American Life*. New York: Harper & Row, 1987.

———. *The Good Society*. New York: Alfred Knopf, 1991.

Berlin, Adele, Mark Zvi Brettler, and Michael Fishbane, eds. *Jewish Study Bible*. New York: Oxford University Press, 2004.

Black, Jim Nelson. *When Nations Die*. Carol Stream, IL: Tyndale House Publishers, 1995.

Blecher, Arthur. *The New American Judaism*. New York: Palgrave Macmillan, 2007.

Bono. *On the Move*. Nashville: Thomas Nelson, 2007.

Borg, Marcus, ed. *Jesus and Buddha*. Berkeley, CA: Ulysses Press, 1997.

Braswell, George. *Islam*. Nashville: Broadman & Holman, 1996.

Bryant, Eric. *Peppermint-Filled Piñatas*. Grand Rapids, MI: Zondervan, 2007.

Buchanan, Patrick. *The Death of the West*. New York: St. Martin's Press, 2002.

Coats, Dan. *Mending Fences*. Grand Rapids, MI: Baker Books, 1990.

Cloud, Henry, and John Townsend. *How People Grow*. Grand Rapids, MI: Zondervan, 2001.

Colson, Charles. *Kingdoms in Conflict*. Grand Rapids, MI: Zondervan, 1987.

Colson, Charles, with Harold Fickett. *The Good Life*. Carol Stream, IL: Tyndale House Publishers, 2005.

Confucius. *The Analects*. Mineola, NY: Dover Publications, 1985.

Dresner, Samuel. *Can Families Survive in Pagan America?* Lafayette, LA: Huntington House Publishers, 1995.

Durant, Will, and Ariel Durant. *The Lessons of History*. New York: Simon & Schuster, 1968.

Easwaran, Eknath, trans., *The Upanishads*. Berkeley, CA: PGW Books, 2007.

Eberle, Gary. *Dangerous Words*. Boston: Trumpeter, 2007.

Eberly, Don. *Restoring the Good Society*. Grand Rapids, MI: Baker Books, 1994.

Eberly, Don, ed. *Building a Healthy Culture*. Grand Rapids, MI: Eerdmans Publishing, 2001.

Eck, Diana. *A New Religious America*. New York: HarperSanFrancisco, 2001.

El-Faizy, Monique. *God and Country*. New York: Bloomsbury USA, 2006.

Emerick, Yahiya. *The Complete Idiot's Guide to Understanding Islam*. Indianapolis: Alpha Books, 2002.

Enroth, Ronald, ed. *A Guide to New Religious Movements*. Downers Grove, IL: InterVarsity Press, 2005.

Gans, Herbert, ed. *Sociology in America*. Newbury Park, CA: Sage Publications, 1990.

Gingrich, Newt. *Real Change*. Washington, D.C.: Regnery Publishing, 2008.

Gomes, Peter. *The Good Life*. San Francisco: HarperSanFrancisco, 2002.

Henderson, Jim. *a.k.a. "Lost."* Colorado Springs: WaterBrook, 2005.

Henry, Carl F. H. *Twilight of a Great Civilization*. Wheaton, IL: Crossway Books, 1988.

Hiebert, Paul. *Transforming Worldviews*. Grand Rapids, MI: Baker Academic, 2008.

Hoffecker, W. Andrew, ed. *Revolutions in Worldview*. Phillipsburg, NJ: P & R Publishing, 2007.

Holmes, Arthur. *Contours of a World View*. Grand Rapids, MI: Eerdmans Publishing, 1983.

Huntington, Samuel. *The Clash of Civilizations and the Remaking of World Order*. New York: Simon & Schuster, 1996.

Hutchison, William. *Religious Pluralism in America*. New Haven, CT: Yale University Press, 2003.

Iacocca, Lee. *Where Have All the Leaders Gone?* New York: Scribner, 2007.

Jacoby, Susan. *The Age of American Unreason*. New York: Pantheon Books, 2008.

Jenkins, Philip. *The Next Christendom*. New York: Oxford University Press, 2002.

Johnson, Haynes. *Divided We Fall*. New York: W. W. Norton & Company, 1995.

Kennedy, Paul. *The Rise and Fall of the Great Powers*. New York: Vintage Books, 1987.

Kertzer, Morris. *What Is a Jew?* New York: Collier Books, 1978.

Kinnaman, David, with Gabe Lyons. *unChristian*. Grand Rapids, MI: Baker Books, 2007.

Kohut, Andrew, John C. Green, Scott Keeter, and Robert C. Toth. *The Diminishing Divide*. Washington, D.C.: Brookings Institution Press, 2000.

Kornfield, Jack, ed. *Teachings of the Buddha*. New York: Bantam Books, 2007.

Kreeft, Peter. *How to Win the Culture War*. Downers Grove, IL: InterVarsity Press, 2002.

Kurtz, Paul, ed. *Humanist Manifestos I and II*. New York: Prometheus Books, 1986.

Life Application Study Bible, New Living Translation. Carol Stream, IL: Tyndale House, 2007.

Luntz, Frank. *Words That Work*. New York: Hyperion, 2007.

Marty, Martin. *The Christian World*. New York: Modern Library, 2008.

Marty, Martin, with Jonathan Moore. *Education, Religion, and the Common Good*. San Francisco: Jossey-Bass, 2000.

Maslow, Abraham. *Religions, Values, and Peak-Experiences*. New York: Penguin Books, 1970.

McLaren, Brian. *A New Kind of Christian*. San Francisco: Jossey-Bass, 2001.

McLaren, Brian, and Tony Campolo. *Adventures in Missing the Point*. Grand Rapids, MI: Zondervan, 2003.

Miller, Barbara Stoller, trans. *The Bhagavad Gita*. New York: Bantam Books, 1986.

Mitchell, Arnold. *The Nine American Lifestyles*. New York: Warner Books, 1983.

Moses, Jeffrey. *Oneness*. New York: Fawcett Books, 1989.

Mukerji, Bithika. *The Hindu Tradition*. New York: Amity House, 1988.

Prothero, Stephen. *American Jesus*. New York: Farrar, Straus, and Giroux, 2003.

Rauf, Imam Feisal Abdul. *What's Right with Islam Is What's Right with America*. San Francisco: HarperSanFrancisco, 2004.

Rosell, Gareth. *The Evangelical Landscape*. Grand Rapids, MI: Baker Books, 1996.

Saliba, John. *Understanding New Religious Movements*. Grand Rapids, MI: Eerdmans, 1995.

Schuessler, Karl. *Measuring Social Life Feelings*. San Francisco: Jossey-Bass, 1982.

Seelye, H. Ned, and Jacqueline Wasilewski. *Between Cultures*. Chicago: NTC Publishing, 1996.

Senge, Peter M., C. Otto Scharmer, Joseph Jaworski, and Betty Sue Flowers. *Presence*. New York: Currency Doubleday, 2004.

Shermer, Michael. *How We Believe*. New York: W. H. Freeman and Company, 2000.

Sire, James. *The Universe Next Door*. Downers Grove, IL: InterVarsity Press, 1997.

Smith, Joseph. *The Book of Mormon*. Salt Lake City: Church of Jesus Christ of Latter-day Saints, 1981.

———. *Pearl of Great Price*. Salt Lake City: Filiquarian Publishing, 2006.

Toynbee, Arnold. *Change and Habit*. Oxford, England: Oneworld Publications, 1992.

Veith, Gene Edward. *Postmodern Times*. Wheaton, IL: Crossway Books, 1994.

Webber, Robert. *Who Gets to Narrate the World?* Downers Grove, IL: InterVarsity Press, 2008.

BIBLIOGRAPHY

Weber, Max. *The Sociology of Religion.* Boston: Beacon Press, 1993.

Wolfe, Alan. *The Transformation of American Religion.* New York: Free Press, 2003.

Wolff, Richard. *The Popular Encyclopedia of World Religions.* Eugene, OR: Harvest House, 2007.

Wuthnow, Robert. *The Restructuring of American Religion.* Princeton, NJ: Princeton University Press, 1988.

ABOUT THE AUTHOR

GEORGE BARNA is the author or coauthor of more than forty books, including best sellers such as *The Frog in the Kettle*, *The Power of Vision*, *Transforming Children into Spiritual Champions*, *Revolution*, and *Pagan Christianity?* He has had more than one hundred articles published in magazines and other periodicals and writes the bimonthly report *The Barna Update* (accessible at http://www.barna.org; subscription is free), which is read by more than a million people each year.

He is the founder and directing leader of The Barna Group, Ltd., a company that provides primary research and resources related to cultural analysis, faith dynamics, and transformation. Through The Barna Group, he has served hundreds of clients as varied as the Billy Graham Association, World Vision, CBN, the Walt Disney Company, Ford Motor Company, Visa USA, and the United States Navy.

He has taught at several universities and seminaries and has served as the teaching pastor of a large, multiethnic church. Barna currently leads a house church. He is a summa cum laude graduate of Boston College and has graduate degrees from Rutgers University and Dallas Baptist University.

He has been married to his wife, Nancy, since 1978, and they live with their three daughters in Southern California. For more information, visit http://www.barna.org.

Available from Barna Books

Committed, born-again Christians are exiting the established church in massive numbers. Why are they leaving? Where are they going? And what does this mean for the future of the church? In this groundbreaking book, George Barna examines the state of the church today—and compares it to the biblical picture of the church as God intended it to be.

How can parents make a lasting impact on the spiritual lives of their children? To find the answer, George Barna researched the lives of thriving adult Christians and discovered the essential steps their parents took to shape their spiritual lives in childhood. *Revolutionary Parenting* shows parents how to instill in their children a vibrant commitment to Christ.

What happens when a Christian hires an atheist to accompany him to church? Find out by following Jim Henderson's journey across the country with skeptic Matt Casper as they visit twelve of America's churches and document their experiences at and reactions to each one. Their eye-opening, entertaining dialogue opens the way for authentic, attentive friendship between Christians and nonbelievers.

Many Christians take it for granted that their church's practices are rooted in Scripture. Yet how do our practices compare to those of first-century believers? *Pagan Christianity?* leads us on a fascinating tour through history that examines and challenges every aspect of the present-day church experience.

BARNA